Benton Rain Patterson

A PRACTICAL GUIDE

THE IOWA STATE

WRITE TO BE READ

TO FEATURE WRITING

UNIVERSITY PRESS / AMES, IOWA

TO MY CHIEF MENTORS: **WESLEY PRICE,** formerly of the

Saturday Evening Post and the *Ladies Home Journal,*

and **LEONARD E. LESOURD,** formerly executive editor of *Guideposts.*

ACKNOWLEDGMENTS. The author and publisher thank the following for permission to reprint:

Guideposts: "Never Listen to Your Fears," by Hubert Humphrey © 1978; "Beginning at the End," by Hamilton Whaley © 1982. By Guideposts Associates, Inc., Carmel, New York 10512.
The North Texas Daily, North Texas State University, Denton, Texas: Story of Jim Petersen, by Fred Welk © 1979.
G. The Magazine of Gainesville: "Here Comes the Garbage Man!" by Terrie Riecke © 1983; "Haven for Hoboes," by Aura Bland © 1983. By the College of Journalism and Communications, University of Florida, Gainesville, Florida 32611.
The Independent Florida Alligator: "Convenience Is in the Eye of the Beholder," by Dave Hogerty © 1981.
Historic Preservation: "Best of the Bed and Breakfasts – The Northeast," by Caskie Stinnett © 1983.
Reader's Digest: "*You Can* Speak in Public," by John Wolfe © 1983.
Baton Rouge Magazine: "1985 Automobiles," by Ellis Sandoz III © 1984.
Journal of Soil and Water Conservation: "Florida's Santa Fe Swamp: To Mine or Not to Mine," by Theresa Waldron © 1983.
The Dallas Morning News: "Police Tipster No Dummy" © 1978.
Boston Magazine: Profile of Joel Meyerowitz by Gerald Peary.
Today (Cocoa, Florida): article by Peter Kerasotis.

First edition, 1986

Library of Congress Cataloging-in-Publication Data

Patterson, Benton Rain, 1929–
    Write to be read: a practical guide to feature writing.

    Includes index.
    1. Feature writing.   I. Title.
PN4784.F37P37   1986   808'.06607044   85–31842
ISBN 0–8138–1943–1

Contents

Preface

I HAD a simple reason for wanting to write a book such as this. It was the same reason I quit, after more than twenty-five years as a writer and editor on newspapers and magazines, my career as an editor to become a classroom teacher in 1977. I wanted to work with young people who were interested in becoming newspaper and magazine journalists, the same thing I was interested in a generation earlier. I wanted to work with the young writers especially.

What I felt I had to offer them was an editor's way of looking at a story, and an editor's experience at getting a writer to deliver what the editor wanted. I also had a resoluteness, no less fixed than the polestar, to do my darnedest to stick to the subject, so that when the subject was How to Write, that's exactly what the instruction would be—not about freelance markets or journalism ethics, choosing an agent, copyright law, not about a lot of other important but tangential subjects. What I wanted to share with the young writers was the meat, not globs of bread stuffing.

I proposed to do so first by letting them know what it is they should be trying to achieve in their writing, and second by showing them how to do it.

Practical and explicit—that's what I wanted, and wanted the book, to be. I wanted to say to the young writer, "Hey, this is the way your editor is going to be thinking. Let's do it like this." Not all editors think alike, of course, but practically all the good ones do.

I tried to include almost everything I thought would help. I especially put into the book something difficult to use in classroom lectures or face-to-face conferences. I put in some examples of what I have been talking about, drawn from a variety of publications and writers. Some examples were written by longtime pros, some by writers who were still college students when they wrote them. Those examples, I felt, would help not only developing writers but also teachers of writing who might use the book as their text for courses in magazine article and feature writing.

I'm sure I haven't said all that could be said on the subject. Many who teach writing, in a classroom or newsroom, will want to add to what's in the book when they face their writers. But I have the feeling I've said enough, since it is intended to be a book for writers in the early stages of their careers, not for everyone up and down the line of writing success.

I believe wholeheartedly in the principles and techniques I've talked about in the book. I know they work. There's not one doubt in my mind that any writer who has the ability and willingness to do it the way the book says will become a noticeably better, more interesting, more effective, more successful writer.

If those results occur, the book will be a success, for it was precisely with those achievements in mind, for able and willing young writers, that I wrote the book.

WRITE TO BE READ

CHAPTER ONE

Can Writing Really Be Taught?

ON THE LAST EVENING of a summer writers conference in Elgin, Illinois, at one of those "ask the experts" sessions, a woman in the audience rose, faced the writing instructors on the dais, among whom I sat, and asked her question in my direction: "Do you think a person can really be taught to write?"

That same question, or something very close to it, had been asked at other such conferences, many times. It had been asked in classrooms and other forums many more times. It's still being asked. It seems the favorite of would-be writers.

Wrapped around the woman's words and the tone in which she spoke them, as obvious as a bandanna about her neck, was her own implicit answer, the usual one: "No, he can't."

The common belief was that writing is something you either can or cannot do. The ability to write is an ineffable mystique, a divine gift, a rare talent. You're born with it or you're not. And what knowledgeable person without guile or deceit would suggest it can be taught, bought, or otherwise ordinarily obtained?

Not me. I started plucking the answer straight from her throat. "Well, not really, of course," I said. "You have to assume that the person. . . ."

When enough of it was out, I turned to a fellow instructor and passed.

"Well," he responded, "there are some *things about* writing that can be taught, but I agree that you can't *actually*. . . ."

AUTHOR'S NOTE: Of all the limitations of our language, surely one of the most frustrating is its inability to include both male and female gender in a singular pronoun. From the women readers of this book, I earnestly ask indulgence when, to avoid clumsiness, I go along with grammatical convention and use the male pronoun to refer to nouns of mixed gender.

That was more than a dozen years ago. Today I would give a different answer. For during the years between then and now, as a magazine editor I've been in a position where I could help guide young writers and have seen several of them achieve such proficiency that they are published in national publications. I have also been a journalism instructor in two state universities and have seen students with no more writing background than a basic reporting course develop into published authors of newspaper features and magazine articles within 16 weeks. I know now that a person *can* be taught to write.

The old answer to the question wasn't exactly wrong, though. Obviously not everyone can learn to write – or write well anyway. Obviously some natural ability is necessary. But just as youngsters who have the appropriate natural talent can be taught to play the piano or tennis well, sooner and better than they would play without a teacher, so can a person be taught to write well enough to be published, read, and enjoyed.

Something else is required. A good teacher. A young newspaper managing editor I know of once told a group of journalism students that he had been a journalism major in college and he knew from his experience that if students didn't know how to write when they entered college, they wouldn't know how to write when they graduated. His statement reflects not a general truth but the competence of *his* instructors.

If it's obvious that not everyone can learn to write, it should also be obvious that not everyone can teach students how to write. But some can, and when an aspiring writer with ability and a teacher with ability come together, something good is bound to result. A good teacher makes a difference in what a student does, whatever the subject, just as a good coach makes a difference in what a team does on the field.

The good writing teacher needs to be a writer himself, experienced at success and failure, knowing all the things that affect writers and their work.

Maybe even more important than being a writer, the good teacher of writing must be a good editor, a handyman with stories and manuscripts, knowing good from bad, recognizing the problems in a piece, and knowing how to solve them. It's never enough simply to criticize; the teacher must tell the learning writer how to fix what's wrong.

Still more, the teacher must know what to say and how to say it to make the learning writer understand what's wrong, why it's wrong, and exactly how it can be made right. He must say it all without crushing the writer or affronting his or her pride. He must say it without causing a loss of confidence in the writer, and without damaging the writer's enthusiasm for the piece.

All the good editors I've known have been writing teachers. They must be to get what they want from writers. Editors who don't teach are the ones who accept anything a writer or reporter turns in, and that's the way their publications read. Good editors are demanding, for their publications' readers and for the publications themselves. Good editors challenge, coax, and teach their reporters and writers to produce what they are demanding.

No textbook or lecture will ever be an adequate substitute for a head-to-head meeting with such a teacher-editor, going over particular problems in particular pieces. Few editors, certainly, would dispute that the best way for anyone to learn to write is to write, have your stuff read and criticized by an editor – then rewrite it and have it read again, and rewrite it again if necessary.

But there are principles that must be learned by all writers, whether they're writing newspaper features, magazine articles, or books. Those principles constitute the fundamentals of good writing and they *can* be taught. Moreover, they can be taught by text or lecture as well as through face-to-face, editor-to-writer communication.

There's nothing especially esoteric about the principles. And the beginning writer needs no special gift to learn them. They're very practical, some even mechanical. They have to do with the way a piece is reported, the kinds of material needed for the piece, and the way the material is organized by the writer and presented to the reader. Those principles are terribly important, however. Every writer of nonfiction – which is what a newspaper feature writer is, and each should see himself as one – absolutely must know, understand, and use those principles in what he writes, every time he writes. The truly gifted writer probably knows them by intuition. The self-taught writer recognizes them in the writing of others and imitates those other writers. The straight-news writer, or reporter, is usually merely a fact arranger and thus can work without the principles.

Every other person who wants to be a writer must be taught those basic principles. That's what this book is intended to do.

CHAPTER TWO

The Great Guiding Principle

THERE IS A PRINCIPLE OF WRITING so important, so fundamental that it can be appropriately called the First Law of Journalism and it is simply this: Be interesting.

The principle is founded on the premise that people will not read something that does not interest them. Or to state it positively: People will read only what they are interested in reading.

Nonfiction writers, of course, are guided by other important considerations, too. Factual accuracy is immensely important in nonfiction writing. Information that purports to be true certainly should be true. The writer needs to get it straight. Clarity is also extremely important. Messages meant to be conveyed by the writer must be so clear and understandable that the reader easily receives them, undistorted and unambiguous. The writer needs to make them clear.

Reader interest, however, is even more important than accuracy and clarity, a statement that might seem, at first thought, a journalistic heresy. Writers – and editors – must realize however that if the reader is not interested enough to read the piece, the accuracy, clarity, and message of the piece will all be lost. The result is the same as if the piece had never been written or published.

The writer's objective is not merely to have written. It's to be read. Journalists write to convey information. They should never assume that because their words are on paper they will be read. They should assume the precise opposite: Their pieces will not be read – unless they're made interesting.

Kinds of Interest

It's obvious that different people, and therefore different readers, are interested in different things. One person may be interested in horse racing; another may have no interest in it whatsoever. One person may be interested in cotton futures; another completely uninterested. The things that affect one's life, or the lives of people close to him, tend to be interesting to him. A cotton broker is interested in the price of cotton futures; a bettor is interested in race results.

The cotton broker may be said to have *pre-existing interest* in cotton futures and in a piece of writing that treats the subject.

The horse race bettor likewise may be said to have pre-existing interest in race results.

Because an individual reader usually has a number of such interests, he brings to his daily newspaper or other publication pre-existing interest in a number of different subjects and thus in a number of different pieces, or stories. Each reader is a potential reader of every piece in the paper, but actually reads only the pieces that interest him. His pre-existing interest determines at least some of those. He reads those pieces because he is interested in the pure information the piece contains, not because of anything special the writer has done in writing the piece. Abstruseness, technical jargon, convoluted syntax, foreign words, disorganization, repetition, and other usually insurmountable barriers to reading prove inconsequential as the reader struggles past them to reach the desired information. A reader's pre-existing interest overcomes all those obstacles.

At the opposite end of the spectrum are pieces about subjects that have absolutely *no interest* for the potential reader. The subject does not concern or touch the reader in any way, and little or nothing can be done to create interest in it.

In between those two extremes of reader interest lies a vast middle ground, stretching from something more than no interest to something less than pre-existing interest. That middle-ground interest may be called *marginal interest*. It is the kind most potential readers have in most pieces. It is *some* interest, an unknown degree which may be enough to propel a reader through an entire article, or not enough to cause him to read the second paragraph.

Raising Reader Interest

The level of reader interest in a subject may change upward or downward as a person matures, changes jobs, moves to a new place, marries, has children, becomes a homeowner, and so forth. Such changes in a potential reader's circumstances can cause shifts in areas of pre-existing interest and no interest. With changed circumstances, an individual may gain pre-existing interest in a subject in which he or she had no interest previously. For example, a man moving from Scranton, Pennsylvania, to Orlando, Florida, might, following his move, acquire pre-existing interest in citrus crops and the effects of cold weather on orange groves, though he had no interest prior to his move.

Such changes in circumstances and resulting changes in reader interest are obviously beyond the control of the writer. A writer cannot order a potential reader moved to Orlando simply to increase his interest in citrus crops. Such changed interest is generated by the individual himself.

However, there are ways to increase reader interest that can be manipulated by other persons. Thus it is possible for Person A to increase Person B's level of interest in a subject or a specific piece of writing. One such way is through a manipulation called *coerced interest*: Person A coerces Person B to have interest in Subject X, Article Y, or Book Z.

When a person is required to read a driver's manual and pass a test before he or she can be issued a driver's license and legally drive an automobile, the interest gained in the driver's manual is coerced interest. When a worker's supervisor instructs him to read a memo on new procedures and institute them immediately, the worker's interest in that memo is coerced interest.

But such coercive power usually doesn't rest in the writer's hands. Writers have to look to their own resources to manipulate reader interest. The manipulation they are able to effect in order to increase the reader's interest in a subject or in a particular piece of writing is called *induced interest*.

Picture three drinking glasses. One is filled with Coca Cola. The second is empty. The third has some Coke in it, less than half a glassful. The first glass, the full one, represents a piece that has pre-existing interest for the reader. The second glass, the empty one, represents a piece that has no interest for the reader. The glass that has some Coke in it represents a piece with marginal interest for the reader.

The problem now is to do something to raise the level of the Coke in that third glass, to the brim if possible. That would be the same as increasing marginal interest to the same level as pre-existing interest. Vendors of Coke in glasses or cups use this trick: Put ice cubes into the glass and the level of the liquid is raised. Writers have some "ice cubes" they can put into the pieces they write, so that the level of reader interest naturally rises. Interest in what they write is thereby induced, causing the reader to *want* to read what the writer has written.

Induced interest is based on the assumption that in addition to those specific subject areas that interest a particular person, there are some things in life that are universally interesting. That is, every reasonably healthy-minded person shares a common interest in certain intangibles. William Randolph Hearst, one of the geniuses and giants of journalism, called them "the fundamentals."

"People," Hearst said, "are interested in the fundamentals—love, romance, adventure, tragedy, mystery."

Hearst's list is probably not exhaustive. There are probably other universally interesting subjects, but the most fundamental object of interest of all, found in any normal person, is self. Every reader is interested in himself or herself. Pieces written to capitalize on the reader's self-interest, a quality which can also be called relevance, will naturally cause reader interest to rise.

Induced interest also derives from the experienced writer's (and editor's) common knowledge that people—potential readers, that is—are interested in other people more than in any other one thing, themselves excepted. About that fact there seems no disagreement.

"There is no doubt about one thing," language scholar Rudolf Flesch says in his book on writing, *The Art of Plain Talk*, "human interest makes for easier reading. Scientific tests have shown that people are better at reading about other people than about anything else."

"If the only people in your newspaper are on the people page, you're reading a dull newspaper," a Gannett newspaper executive, Joseph M. Ungaro, told his fellow editors. "People are what news is all about."

"Readers are more interested in people than in ideas or issues," Jean Block, articles editor of *Good Housekeeping*, told a group of journalism teachers.

"Stories," according to Reuven Frank, NBC documentary maker and president of NBC News, "succeed to the degree that they are about people—not about things which 'affect' people or 'involve' people, but about the individual people themselves."

Gene Roddenberry, creator of the "Star Trek" television series, said, "Dramatic excitement invariably comes out of stories about people."

Why other people are so interesting may have been explained by S. I. Hayakawa, the semanticist and scholar who became a United States senator from California. "All literary and dramatic enjoyment," he says, "appears to involve to some degree the reader's imaginative identification of himself with one or more of the roles portrayed and his projection of himself into the situations described in the story." That's important for every writer to remember. If it's true, moreover, readers are interested in other people because they like to put themselves into the other guy's shoes, which is perhaps another expression of self-interest.

Rudolf Flesch, who made a career out of studying people's reading habits, offered another explanation of people's interest in other people. It is, he says, "probably because man knows nothing so well as man. His thinking and his language started out as simple talk about what he and people around him were doing."

Whatever the explanation for it is, it is a generally accepted fact that what a writer writes is more interesting when he puts people into it. The manipulation then to increase reader interest involves the writer's capitalizing on the phenomenon of people's interest in other people.

The learning writer's task becomes more specific when, after recognizing he must put people into his pieces, he asks himself, "How do I do it? How can I incorporate people and the fundamentals into what I write?"

The answer is probaby best given by repeating what Norman Vincent Peale said when he described on one occasion what he believed to be the world's most effective form of communication. "It can be summed up," Peale said, "in four words: TELL ME A STORY."

By telling a story, a writer is able to introduce people as well as Hearst's fundamentals into what he writes. He is able to convey his information to the reader in a way that actually increases the reader's interest in the subject and in the particular piece.

The editors of the *Reader's Digest* and *Time* told Rudolf Flesch the same thing.

> I asked one of the *Reader's Digest* editors how they came by their easy, readable style. There was no special recipe, he said, they just naturally wrote—or edited—that way. But he added something else that was far more revealing. "Whenever we want to draw attention to a problem," he said, "we wait until somebody does something about it. Then we print the story of how he did it."
>
> I also asked *Time* magazine about *its* readability formula. Again, I didn't get much of an answer. "Writers are instructed," I was informed, "to make their stories as complete, as readable, and as interesting as possible. Of course, the language of *Time* is the idiom of American speech. We try to render concrete, vivid, and human all the events on which we report, and consistent with that effort is the clear language of a spoken idiom." A little later, however, in *Time's* twenty-fifth anniversary issue, I got a much clearer answer in print: "The basis of good *Time* writing is narrative, and the basis of good narrative is to tell events (1) in the order in which they occur; (2) in the form in which an observer might have seen them—so that readers can imagine themselves on the scene. A *Time* story must be *completely* organized from beginning to end; it must go from nowhere to somewhere and sit down when it arrives."
>
> And that's the secret of America's two largest factual magazines. They print stories. Why? Because only stories are really readable.

Putting information into story form can be called storytelling; and when the nonfiction writer does it, the piece usually contains ample amounts of characterization, dialogue, description, and narrative.

Characterization means enough information about characters so the reader feels he knows them. Dialogue is what the characters say and think. Description is the details necessary for the reader to recreate in his mind, through the use of language, what his senses would have perceived had he been an eyewitness to the reality that occurred and about which the writer is writing. Narrative is the telling itself, the written account that relates the reality that occurred, the description of the action that took place.

Storytelling devices have also been called fiction techniques, and a style of nonfiction writing that became popular in the 1960s made extensive use of so-called fiction techniques. The use of storytelling to convey truth and information, however, is at least as old as the Genesis account of creation.

Tom Wolfe, the writer who in the late 1960s used storytelling devices in writing newspaper features and magazines articles, became a spokesman for the "new" style of nonfiction writing, which was labeled "the new journalism." Others using more or less the same style included Gay Talese, Jimmy Breslin, Rex Reed, George Plimpton, and perhaps most notably, Truman Capote, whose book *In Cold Blood* was promoted by its publisher as a "nonfiction novel."

Touting and explaining "the new journalism" in the foreword to an anthology of examples of the style, Wolfe identifies the four writing devices that, he claims, novelists have used to hold their readers and that the new journalism adopted: (1) scene-by-scene construction; (2) dialogue; (3) third-person point of view, a device which allows the writer to present every scene through the eyes, and sometimes the voice, of a particular character; and (4) symbolic detail. Wolfe's analysis, moreover, implies narrative as another device used both in novels and in the new journalism, for the four other devices cannot be employed without narrative.

A writer doesn't need to use all those devices to increase reader interest through storytelling. In fact, not all the writers Wolfe recognized as practitioners of the new journalism used the devices. But a knowledge of them gives a writer better understanding of the elements needed to build interesting pieces of writing, the kind that induces reader interest.

To test the theory that reader interest is raised by using storytelling devices, I once conducted an experiment with students at North Texas State University. Fifty-six students were given different pieces of text to read. Half read Text A, written in inverted-pyramid style (the standard newswriting way of arranging facts in a descending order of importance) without narrative or other storytelling devices. The other half read Text B, containing the same basic information as Text A, but using storytelling devices. No photos or other illustrations, titles, headlines, or other display elements were included with the text.

The students were asked to rate how interesting they found the text: (1) interesting, (2) somewhat interesting, (3) not interesting, or (4) very dull. The ratings were subjective, of course, but subjectivity is the nature of reader interest.

Among those who read Text A, the inverted-pyramid version, 57.2 percent rated it as either interesting or somewhat interesting. Among those who read Text B, with storytelling devices, 86 percent said it was interesting or somewhat interesting.

The test showed that the "ice cubes" had done their job. The storytelling devices had made the piece interesting to 50 percent more readers.

Importance of Reader Interest
to Newspaper Journalism

In 1977 the American Society of Newspaper Editors commissioned Yankelovich, Skelly & White, a research organization, to survey newspaper readers and report on what the readers thought about their newspapers. The findings included a statement that editors and writers might have perceived all along but had failed to do much about: "Television newswatching is passive; magazines are entertainment and easy to read; newspapers are hard work."

The fact that readers believe reading a newspaper constitutes hard work may explain declining newspaper readership in America. According to one researcher, newspaper circulation per household has been declining in the United States since about 1910. Further *The Wall Street Journal* has reported that newspaper sales nationwide have trailed population growth since 1959.

Other studies indicate that the circulation decline cannot be blamed on rising subscription prices. A survey of newspaper readers conducted by the Gannett Company, the nation's biggest owner of newspapers, concluded that "price was not a deterrent to readership. But it can be a catalyst to stop reading when combined with other sources of dissatisfaction."

One such source of dissatisfaction, possibly the greatest, was identified by Carolyn E. Burke, a professor of education at Indiana University and an authority on reading, when she spoke of the writing and editing faults of newspapers. "If newspaper people do not look upon the reading process as pleasant and write and edit accordingly, they cannot expect to find pleasure in reading newspapers . . . ," she said. "If readers do not find pleasure in their newspapers, the fault lies in the selection of content and the craftsmanship of writing."

Literary critic Stuart Chase returned the same indictment. "When the audience turns away," he said, "there is something wrong with the writer's communication line. He should look to his tools."

Readers must be wooed and won by the writer. Writers—and editors—must recognize the importance of making their publications interesting, of making readers *want* to read them. The historic role of the American newspaper as the major source of news and the foremost influence on public opinion might be at stake.

Elements of Good Writing: The Parts of the Piece

EVERY EVENING George Barrett kisses his four sons goodnight, including the two oldest who are 17 and 19. It embarrasses the older boys to be kissed by their father, and he admits that it may seem "a little weird." But, he says, "I think that the way I live I may never see them again, and I don't want to be stretched out dying in a street some place wishing for one more chance to see my family and say goodby. So every time I kiss them it's like it's the last time I'll ever see them, and I'm kissing them goodby forever."

That is the first paragraph of an article James Mills wrote for *Life*. In it are all the storytelling devices: characterization, dialogue, description, and narrative. The reader is introduced to George Barrett and sees him do something that reveals his character or personality. The reader also hears him speak, again revealing something about him. The things about Barrett that are revealed to the reader constitute characterization; the reader starts to know George Barrett and begins to identify with him.

What Barrett says constitutes dialogue, even though he is the only one who speaks. The words that show Barrett in action, doing something—"Every evening George Barrett kisses his four sons goodnight"—constitute narrative. The reader also gets some description—words that, in that paragraph, let the reader *see* something: the two older sons are 17 and 19 years old. They're older teen-agers, not grade-school kids, not middle-aged men with children of their own. The reader does not not see George Barrett yet. His picture comes in Mills's second paragraph:

Forever can come very suddenly to Detective George Barrett. He is a hunter of men. And none of those he hunts – thieves, drug pushers, Murphy men, assault and robbery men, killers – wants to confront him on anything resembling even terms. Because when George Barrett hunts for a man, he invariably finds him; and when he finds him, the man is not always arrested, but he is always sorry he was found. George Barrett is a tough cop. His eyes, cold as gun metal, can be looked at but not into. His jaw is hard and square as a brick, and his thin lips are kept moist by nervous darting passes of his tongue. When he laughs, only his face and voice laugh. Inside, George Barrett does not laugh.

Now the reader sees him. The reader has discovered who George Barrett is and what kind of man he is. The reader is also identifying more with Barrett, beginning to place himself in Barrett's shoes. All of that is happening because of the characterization, dialogue, and description supplied by the writer.

Everything Mills has written so far about Barrett can be classified into four categories, the same categories into which virtually all written language can be classified. Everything a writer wants to write can be constructed with those four components; nothing more is needed. They are the building blocks, and it's immensely important for a writer to know them, their functions, and how to use them.

Using the Four Building Blocks

NARRATIVE. Narrative describes *action*; therefore all the words and sentences that *show* movement, show what is happening or did happen, can be labeled *narrative*. Narrative is what lets the reader see, in his mind, the action occurring – the same way movie film lets the viewer see action with his eyes. Every viewer knows how boring a talky or purely scenic movie can be; it's the action that makes it interesting. The same is true for a feature or article. Narrative is the building block a writer uses to put action into what he writes.

Here's a sample of narrative from a piece Ronald B. Taylor wrote for the *Los Angeles Times*:

Night darkened the cab as Kathy Manning downshifted the big, 18-wheeler and pulled off the freeway, queuing up behind other trucks at the Castaic, Calif., scales along Interstate 5.

She let the 72,500-pound semi-tractor and trailer roll slowly across the scales, got the green clearance light for the load of metal ceiling grids and gunned the powerful diesel.

Checking her mirrors for oncoming traffic, she wheeled the rig onto the freeway. As she shifted up through the gears, Manning yelled over the engine's roar: "If I ever meet a man I can love, I'll settle down, quit drivin' truck."

She took a pinch of snuff, tucked it between her lower lip and gums and continued, "But this is something I can do. I've mastered it. I'm a truck driver and I like it."

Except for the quotes, label that whole section narrative. It shows the action.

DESCRIPTION. In reality (as opposed to an account of reality, written after the action has occurred and passed into history) the human senses perceive sounds, sights, smells, feelings, and tastes. Language gives names to each of those perceptions (*screech, whisper, prairie, shoe, new-mown hay, putrid, smooth, icy, sour, salty*), and when the names of those perceptions are read by a reader who shares the writer's language, the reader's mind conjures up the appropriate perceptions. The names, or words, are symbols of little pieces of reality.

Description is what lets the reader see for himself, in effect, what an actual eyewitness saw. It lets the reader smell, feel, taste, and hear, through language, what his senses would have perceived had he been there. It will also be referred to in this book as *descriptive detail.*

The task of a writer is to permit the reader to experience—vicariously, through language—the reality that occurred, as if the reader had been there when the action was going on. The task is to make the reader feel, while he is reading, that the reality *is* occurring and that he is living in it. The reader is thus transported from his safe and distant seat to the spot where the action is occurring.

Here's a sample of description from an article by David Hellerstein that ran in *Esquire:*

It's a chilly December day; the Manhattan sky is dull, the pavement free of snow. I leave my hosptial at midmorning, wearing a white coat, beeper on my belt. I cross the street and enter Memorial Sloan-Kettering Cancer Center and hurry past the security guard—just another doctor late for a meeting.

Dr. Lewis Thomas's office is off a corridor of laboratories in a research building in the block-square medical complex. The secretary announces me. I wait, watching a pallid woman proofread *Blood* journal galleys, sliding a metal rule down long pages. I shiver. From Thomas's office comes a high-pitched boyish voice, laughing into the telephone, wild and crackling:

"... wouldn't it be better if they were *married?*"

Then Thomas appears.

Six feet tall, of solid build, wearing a conservative suit—at first glance Lewis Thomas is more the banker or corporate lawyer than the man of science. His graying hair is brushed up and to the right. He wears horn-rimmed glasses. His face, deeply lined, is lively yet fundamentally serious. He moves quickly, a little stiff in the shoulders as though trying not to jar a sensitive organ. Up close there's some gleam in his eyes.

That's description.

QUOTES. Quotes are the same as dialogue, except that they don't include thoughts (as in: *What a dumb thing to do!* she thought). Quotes is the word more commonly and comfortably used by newspaper editors and reporters. Quotes are used to recreate the words spoken during the reality that occurred. They are what was said, presented in quotation marks so the reader hears, in effect, the speaker himself say it. Quotes further allow the reader to be on the scene. They also allow voices other than the narrator's (the writer is the narrator when he or she is telling a story in third person). Quotes also contribute to characterization, allowing readers to feel as if they know the character.

"Realistic dialogue," according to Tom Wolfe, "involves the reader more completely than any other single device. It also establishes and defines character more quickly and effectively than any other single device." It's important to notice that Wolfe said *realistic* dialogue. What is quoted for the reader must sound, in the reader's mind, like the actual person talking, as in this scene from a first-person article by Elizabeth Kaye, which ran in *California* magazine:

He played the jukebox. He played Pac-Man. Usually he hardly drank at all, but now he drank too much. He started several conversations with the question, "What kind of music do you like?" He was having a wonderful time in these surroundings that reminded him of his past, and I had never felt so distanced from him. While he was playing pool, one of the girls approached him.

"Are you an actor?" she asked.

"I'm a writer," said Tony.

"What kind of writer?"

"Right now I'm writing a story about Jonathan Winters."

"Well," I said in the car going home, "I've had a wonderful time, but this wasn't it."

"You're hard to please," he said.

"I just don't like bars. To tell you the truth, I wish you wouldn't go to them."

"To tell *you* the truth, if you start telling me where I can go, I'll leave."

"You mean you'd choose bars over me?"

"I'd choose myself over you."

I didn't say anything for a moment. "You're pretty smart for such a young guy," I said finally.

He put his arm around me. He said teasingly, "Now tell me what you don't like about bars."

"First of all, they're a waste of time."

"What else?"

"They're coeducational."

He laughed. "I knew it. What else?"

"They're so low class."

"I *am* low class," he said.

The words in the quote marks are true dialogue. They constitute conversation. Quotes may be dialogue—conversation that occurred and is recreated by the writer—or they may be isolated remarks by the speaker, remarks made to himself, to a reporter, to God, to no one in particular. Quotes are simply what was said.

Here's a sample from a feature on Haitian refugees Mike Winerip did for the *Miami Herald:*

Simon stood and took Calixte's hands toward the end of the visit. This was Simon's prayer: "Lord, you are the father to everyone on land. This is your people, and I'm your people also. This boy, he didn't do nothing wrong. He didn't kill nobody. I don't see how you punish a boy in a situation like that. So

please, Father Lord, let him go out. I
praise you again and again."

When he was done, Simon opened
his eyes and kissed Calixte on each

cheek.

"Thank you very much, brother-in-law," said Calixte.

Here's another example from Ronald Taylor's piece on the woman
truck driver:

Once when she thought about quitting, she applied for a clerk-typist job with the Los Angeles Police Department.

"I passed all the tests, went in there and I watched those clerk-typists at work for a while, then I turned and walked out. That kind of work's not for me," she said.

Quotes differ from quotations. Quotations are eternal phrases prepared in advance of their being spoken ("Four score and seven years ago. . . ."; "Ask not what your country can do for you. . . ."; ". . . a day that will live in infamy. . . ."). Quotations are meant to be chiseled into marble. Quotes, however, are the way real people actually talk. They sound real; they *are* real. Quotes that don't sound real or that seem stilted are called wooden quotes and should be avoided whenever possible.

EXPOSITION. Exposition is explanation. It is the writer speaking, not in words that *show* something to the reader, but in words that *tell* the reader about something. Here is an example from an article about hunting wild hogs, by Thomas McIntyre, which ran in *Sports Afield:*

In the Old World, of course, the wild boar was among the greatest animals of the chase. Records of boar hunts can be found in cave paintings 40,000 years old. The Assyrians, Egyptians, Greeks and Romans all left behind images in art of the hunt for the boar. In literature, the fifth-century B.C. Athenian essayist, Xenophon, in his hunting treatise *Cynegeticus*, recommended that the Greek boar hunter use a spear with a 15-inch blade "keen as a razor," and with copper teeth projecting from the middle of the socket to stop the boar from running up the length of the shaft when struck and held by the hunter. He also advised the use of "Indian, Cretan, Locrian and Laconian" hounds, "prepared to fight the beast." The boar was to be driven from its lair and caught in a purse net. But if it escaped before being killed and attacked a hunter who was without benefit of a spear, that hunter was to hurl himself to the ground and grasp the underbrush to prevent the boar from getting its tusks underneath him and ripping his belly.

Another example, from *The New Yorker:*

Writers, artists, and intellectuals in Yugoslavia—probably to a greater extent than those in other Eastern European countries—must contend with bewildering, kaleidoscopic shifts in degrees of freedom and constraint. For the most part, they respond to attack with boldness or bravura, but when subjected to concerted criticism they adopt an attitude of quiet withdrawal which can last weeks or even months. During such times, they are seen but not heard, and they float about town like martyred or tormented spirits waiting to be liberated.

It is virtually impossible for writers to avoid using exposition, no matter what kind of piece they are writing. Some things simply must be explained to the reader: background, circumstances, procedures, reasons, and so forth. Exposition can help speed up the story (that is, tell it more quickly). A writer must constantly realize, however, that exposition, of all the elements of the piece, is the dullest and hardest to read — therefore it is the part most likely to repel the reader.

The tendency of too many writers, especially newspaper writers, is to tell all, explain all, with exposition. They don't take time to recreate the action, the scene, the dialogue. They simply summarize for the reader and, in so doing, write as if they don't care if the piece is read or not. It's as if they don't want to be bothered with repeating the detail for the reader. The reader is held at arm's length while the writer selfishly enjoys the detail for himself.

The writer's function is not to absorb detail for himself or herself, then merely explain and summarize it for the reader. The writer should loop his arm over the reader's shoulders and say, "Hey, I've got something to show you" — then *show* the reader. Exposition does *not* show; it explains and tells. Therefore it should be used only when absolutely necessary. It should come in small doses when it is used, so that bits of exposition are quickly followed by bigger bits of the interesting parts of the piece: narrative, descriptive detail, and quotes. For example, in that article about wild hogs, author McIntyre immediately follows his exposition section with narrative:

Now darkness was almost upon us. Before the last of the shooting light on the hunt's second day, Ellis, August and I had spend most of an hour sitting far up on one side of a canyon, silently watching two enormous boars stir in the thick black sage on the other. The pigs would show us only the tops of their black backs, or their rumps moving behind bush, so we never had a shot. Smaller pigs had come out into the open draw below us to begin the feeding that would carry them from evening through the night and to barely past dawn. But Ellis was set firmly on a trophy. When the big boars got into the sage so thick we could no longer see any sign of them, we climbed out of the canyon and back up to the ridge to start our way in, leaving the boars for another time.

We were halfway down the ridge, with its oaks and pines, when we saw the herd of wild pigs out in the open field below us. They stood in the cold shadow the ridge cast in the sunset, nearly a dozen animals, all large adults. The largest stood alone at the rear of the herd, tall and lean-looking, his thick mane of bristles caping his neck and shoulders. We worked our way down the slope in silence to where Ellis could get a rest for his rifle.

What It Takes to Make a Story

In newspaper jargon any piece can be, and usually is, called a *story*. It might be a straight news story, feature story, sports story, wedding story, page-one story, breaking story, anything. Story is the general term applied to practically any piece of content. In this book, however, story means the account, the re-creation through words, of an event or incident or happening. It is a story in the same way that *Moby Dick, The Wizard of Oz, Catcher in the Rye,* and *Gone With the Wind* are stories—except that our stories are factual, not fictional. They are tales, but true ones.

Every story, fiction or nonfiction, must have certain elements. Without them, it is either not a story at all, or it is a poor one. The necessary elements are: characters, action, and description.

CHARACTERS. A story must be about at least one character. Ordinarily characters are humans, but they don't have to be. They may be animals or even inanimate objects *if* the writer gives them human characteristics. (*Steve the Steam Shovel* and *The Little Engine That Could* are children's books that tell stories using inanimate objects as characters. Charlotte the spider of *Charlotte's Web,* Black Beauty, and the rabbits of *Watership Down* are some animals that have served as story characters.)

ACTION. Action is what the characters do, say, or think. Characters must *do* something, providing action for the reader to see and hear.

DESCRIPTION. Description lets the reader see not only the character but what the character looks like, what he's wearing, how old he is, what kind of car he drives, where he works, where he lives, the scene where the action occurred, the night, the rain, the cold—all the important details the reader's senses would have perceived had he been there while the action was occurring. It's possible to have a story without including description. But it's a more interesting story when description is in it.

There are other desirable but not essential elements that may be added to a story to make it more interesting, more significant, more memorable: plot (or story line), suspense, conflict, change (whereby one or more characters undergoes a change in understanding, attitude, condition, etc.), and climax. When they are a part of the reality, a feature writer should put them into a piece. If they are not part of the reality, there is no way they can be included. To do so would turn fact into fiction.

Using Stories

To take advantage of what we know about readers' interest in other people and in the things William Randolph Hearst called "the fundamentals," a feature writer deliberately puts people (characters) into what he writes. He describes them and shows them (description) doing and saying (action, expressed through narrative and quotes) whatever it is that makes the characters worth writing – and reading – about. When he puts those elements into his piece, a writer is ipso facto *featurizing* his subject, handling his material and writing his piece as a feature. He is also telling a story, which you now know is the best and most effective way to convey information. The writer thereby gives his piece and his publication the best possible chance of being read.

Sometimes a piece, instead of containing several little stories, will be one long story. The writer will spend the entire piece telling one story. That kind of piece is called *continuous narrative*. It can be the simplest sort of piece to report and write. When he gathers his information for it, the writer merely keeps asking, in effect, "And then what happened?" When writing the piece, he simply picks a good spot to start the action, interrupts it for background and explanation (one of the necessary exposition sections of the piece), then resumes the chronological account of what happened.

Usually, however, a piece will *not* be continuous narrative. The piece will cover some subject other than a single event or a narrow span of time – the two major types of subjects that lend themselves to continuous narrative. Instead of being continuous narrative, the usual piece will be built around two or more small stories that might run in length from a couple of paragraphs to a couple of pages of copy. Those little stories are called *anecdotes*. They are not necessarily funny, although they might be. They might also be grim, sad, poignant, hateful, or whatever else the reality which they recreate was.

Anecdotes are stories because they contain all the elements needed to make a story: characters, action, description. And sometimes more. In all of prose's forms, components, and styles, there is nothing more important to reader interest or delightful to the reader than anecdotes. They are to a piece of writing what flesh is to the human form.

The ability to handle anecdotal material – the story elements from which anecdotes are made – is so important that it can be considered the key to success for a nonfiction writer. Unless he learns to write with anecdotes, a writer will reach a stage of arrested growth and never develop beyond it.

Experienced writers have found at least four good uses for anecdotes, and every other writer should make those same discoveries. He should learn to use anecdotes:

To introduce the subject to the reader. Notice in the James Mills excerpt at the beginning of this chapter how Mills shows the reader a scene, puts characters into it, shows the main character doing something, and lets him speak. The lead is a little story about George Barrett, whom the reader meets for the first time. (See Chapter 6 for more on anecdotal leads.)

To illustrate or make the point. It's not enough for a writer to make a general statement to the reader, even if it's attributed. A generalization (for example: "Harold Coogan often draws on his own brand of Irish wit") should always be supported with a specific, offered as evidence of the truth of the generalization. In the case of the Harold Coogan generalization, the writer should follow it with an anecdote (or a quote) showing Coogan being witty.

Here are two examples from a *McCall's* article by Susan Jacoby, showing how anecdotes support generalizations:

Bearing in mind the slow progression through the stages of grief, it is important to be willing to listen to the bereaved long after the initial loss. "I wasn't able to talk about my wife at all for the first few months after her death," says one man, "and then a flood of memories was released when I saw a dress in a department-store window that was exactly the kind she used to like. About nine months after she died, I began to want to talk about her and our married life—but my relatives thought this was morbid. I'll never forget spending a whole evening with one of my wife's friends, reminiscing about a wonderful vacation that we all had taken years ago. It wasn't morbid at all—we were remembering her life instead of her death."

. . . When some bereaved people find that they are begining to take pleasure in life again, they may deliberately sabotage their own prospects for happiness.

One woman, who had become seriously interested in a man three years after her husband's death, ruined the relationship by fleeing—with no explanation to the man—to the small town in Vermont where she had spent her honeymoon. When she returned a month later, the man had started seeing someone else. At that point, an understanding friend suggested that she might benefit from counseling.

The use of anecdotes to illustrate or make the point is a communication device as old as antiquity. Jesus used them to teach his followers. His anecdotes are called parables. They are just as effective today as they ever were. "The anecdote that makes the point," according to Hubert Luckett, longtime editor of *Popular Science* and later editorial vice president of Times-Mirror Magazines, "is the best way to communicate."

To condense a long story. A story that in reality occurred over many months or even years can be told within the restrictions of limited space by relating significant incidents, or episodes, told as anecdotes. Episodes about certain key characters in the ancestry of writer Alex Haley constituted the telling of the generations-long story of how one man came to be who he was and where he was. Haley's book, *Roots,* was first a magazine serial, then a book, then a television serial. The same technique can be applied to much shorter pieces. Curtis Hartman, in his article in *Inc.* magazine, did something similar by showing episodes in the lives of John and Peter Van Arsdale and their troubled airline, Provincetown-Boston Airline. He used episodic anecdotes to help compress action that occurred over many months.

On paper, the rise of John Van Arsdale ended with a single flight. On November 29, 1983, according to the FAA, he had been flying a Martin 404 from Hyannis, Mass., to Naples when he lost all the hydraulic fluid just after takeoff. Rather than landing the plane at once, as required by the FAA, he had flown on to Jacksonville, Fla., where PBA has a maintenance base. In Jacksonville, he moved the passengers onto a Nihon YS-11, and flew down to Naples. Since he had never won an FAA rating on a YS-11, he was flying illegally. Then, when the trip was completed, he had forged another pilot's signature on the flight log. . . .

Peter had given a lot of thought to running a managers' meeting, even before he became CEO. He had always thought John was too critical, too much like their father. His meetings were hour after hour of finger pointing, with no agenda and no objective. So Peter sat quietly, drumming his fingers on his desk as his managers had their say one by one. Having the CEO's ear was a new experience for most of them, and they took it—at length. What should have been a half-hour meeting stretched on to two hours, because every decision was deferred to Peter. We need 200 copies of the manuals—what printer should we use? The pilots would be testing at the airport—what

motel should they stay in?

In time, Peter hoped, he would be able to avoid so much detail. But for now his managers needed all the support they could get. "I've got a lot of guys in there who are really trying to watch the dollars, and I've got guys in there who have never had to make decisions." He knew how they felt. . . .

John himself came to the office only once that week.

Time had stopped for John with decertification. He looked tan and relaxed, but the threat of a legal battle dragged on, and his 63-year-old mother worried about what he would do with himself. His plans were vague. Write a book? Move to France? Run for office? In the meantime, he had a house filled with long-deferred projects to keep him occupied, and lunches with his son at McDonald's. He had come by the office to pick up a few personal effects, and to see if he could borrow his brother's boat.

"Sure," Peter agreed. "I could only use it between midnight and six in the morning anyway."

Then he stood with John in his new office, looking at seat fabric for the new planes until his brother was ready to go.

"Anything I can do to help?" John asked.

"Nope," Peter said.

The same kind of condensation can be done in 1000 to 1200 words, a normal newspaper feature length.

To conclude the piece. In a feature, unlike a straight news story, the conclusion is almost as important as the lead. When a reporter writes an inverted-pyramid news story, he often doesn't know what the last paragraph will be when the story appears in print. In fact, that's one reason the writer writes it in inverted-pyramid style, so an editor or a production person can whack it off at almost any point below the second paragraph.

The feature, however, should be a rounded story. The writer should plan it – plan how it will begin, where it will go from there, how it will end. If the writer does the job well, the reader will be drawn gradually, more deeply into the piece until finally the story has been told and the reader recognizes the end without having to be signalled by a 30-dash or some other graphic device. The piece should neither peter out nor stop abruptly. It should conclude with something that sums up or makes the final statement, or otherwise rounds off the piece. Such a conclusion is often provided by an appropriate anecdote.

James Mills used such an anecdote to conclude and round off his piece on Detective Barrett. After letting the reader see, hear, and feel the problems and frustrations of a big city cop's job, the main message of the piece, Mills offered a concluding anecdote to sum up both Barrett and the situation:

So Barrett thinks about America's less sophisticated areas "where people still know the difference between the cops and the robbers." He is in a motel talking to the security man when a report comes in that a guest has been burglarized. Barrett and the security man go to the room. Someone has entered the room while the guest, a Wyoming businessman, and his wife and little boy were out sight-seeing. The burglar took exactly $2.17.

Barrett and the house detective leave the room and as they walk to the elevator the house man says disgustedly, "What about that? A crummy $2.17 and he wants to make a big federal case out of it."

"No, no, you're wrong," Barrett says. "He's from Wyoming and someone was in *his* room. That's what got him mad. And I subscribe to that completely. We're beginning to take this stuff for granted. 'Someone in my room? Oh, okay.' Like it was the standard thing. Well, it shouldn't be the standard thing. I'm with the man from Wyoming. He's one of the good guys – and there aren't too many of us left."

Using Quotes and Description
Outside the Context of the Action

Quotes may be used to recreate conversation or other words spoken during the action the narrative describes, as when Barrett says, "He's one of the good guys – and there aren't too many of us left." Quotes may also be used outside the context of the action described, as when Barrett says in the first paragraph of the piece, "I think that the way I live I may never see them again, and I don't want to be stretched out dying in a street some place wishing for one more chance to see my family." Barrett makes those comments not as he kisses his four sons good night, but after the incident, outside the context of the action.

Quotes outside the context of the action allow comment, background, and explanation without having to resort to exposition. The explanation comes from another's voice, not the writer's. Quotes outside the action also allow the characters to speak for themselves, just as quotes do when they are spoken within the context of the action. They also allow the reader to hear voices other than the narrator's.

Quotes outside the context of the action may also be used to support a generalization, in the same way an anecdote does. For example, the statement about Harold Coogan may be supported by an anecdote, by recreating an incident and including something Coogan said during the incident, or it may be supported by one or more quotes from Coogan, apart from the incident. The quotes would simply let him speak, and the reader would "hear" him, but there would be no scene or action.

A writer, however, must be careful about mixing quotes that occur outside the action with those that occur during the action. In most cases, outside-the-action quotes should not be inserted into an anecdote or continuous narrative where they may interrupt the scene and action being recreated. They can spoil the illusion of reality that a writer works hard to create.

Here's an example of how the illusion is lost through misuse of an outside-the-action quote:

Dr. Llew Ehrhart and two of his colleagues walked over the white, sandy dunes, finally arriving on the hard-packed and damp sand of the seashore. It was barely light; the sun hadn't yet broken the horizon.

A green mound down the beach caught Ehrhart's eye, and he started toward it. Reaching the object, Ehrhart froze. It was a green turtle.

"I remember thinking, *Not another!*" he said. "His back fin looked bitten to pieces, but he was still alive."

Ehrhart immediately ran back to his small pickup truck and carefully drove it over the dunes. He and his colleagues hoisted the turtle with nets into the bed of the truck, then sped off to try to save the turtle's life.

Notice how the quote that begins "I remember thinking . . .," breaks into the chronology. Ehrhart is speaking to the reporter in an outside-the-action quote, weeks after the incident. The writer should have written it this way:

A green mound down the beach caught Ehrhart's eye, and he started toward it. Reaching the object, Ehrhart froze. It was a green turtle.

Not another! he thought. Its back fin .

looked as if it had been bitten to pieces, but the turtle was still alive. Ehrhart immediately ran back to his small pickup truck and . . .

Unless a writer is attempting some attainable special effect, or unless there is some other good and cogent reason for doing otherwise, quotes outside the action should be delivered to the reader only following the anecdote (or in some cases before it), never in it.

Description may also be used outside the action. James Mills did so in his description of Detective Barrett (see page 15). The reader gets to see Barrett, but not in any particular scene. It's a still picture the reader sees of Barrett, not a movie.

Summary

Each of the four parts of a piece — narrative, description, quotes, and exposition — is necessary to help deliver the intended message. Furthermore, it is important to pace a piece so that the parts work together successfully. This lead from a feature by Bella Stumbo of the *Los Angeles Times* shows how it is possible to mix them into a readable whole:

Yvonne and Yvette were standing in front of a mirror in their bedroom, intently combing their hair. They constantly fiddle with their hair, which rarely seems to please them. — *Narrative*

They were dressed in matching jeans and striped, scoop-neck T-shirts, — *Description*

which they step into. They always dress identically because, said Yvonne, — *Exposition*

"Otherwise we'd look awkward." — *Quote (outside the context of the action)*

"My hair's too short," grumped — *Quote (within the context of the action)*

Yvette, who had been to the hair- — *Exposition*

dresser the day before. "I went to some new place, and I shouldn't have." — *Quote (within the context)*

The twins always speak in the singular, never the plural. It can be disconcerting at first. — *Exposition*

"Mine's too curly," said Yvonne. "I think I'll get it straightened some." — *Quote (within the context)*

They combed in silence for a time, two combs, four hands, four elbows busily churning in the air. — *Narrative*

Asked finally how they determine whose hair is whose, Yvonne's hands hardly skipped a lick. — *Narrative*

"It's simple. Here, I'll show you," — *Quote (within the context)*

she said, still peering at herself in the mirror. With a practiced flick of the wrist, she drew an arbitrary part across the long, continuous crown that connects her to her sister. — *Narrative*

"*That* hair," she said solemnly, pointing to the far side of the line, "is *her* hair, and *this* hair," she said, pointing to the near side of the line, "is my hair." — *Quote (within the context) and narrative*

Yvonne and Yvette Jones of Los Angeles are the only surviving adult Siamese twins who are still joined, medical records show. ⎤—*Exposition*

As a feature writer you need to remember only a few simple rules to make what you write interesting to the reader: (1) Put specific people into the piece, (2) tell stories, and (3) let the reader see and hear for himself. Every feature or article must have ample amounts of the elements of good writing: anecdotes, quotes, and descriptive detail. Exposition is as dull as a sermon and should be used only when absolutely necessary.

The All-Important Interview

ANECDOTES, QUOTES, DESCRIPTIVE DETAIL—all the other specifics that form the substance of an article or feature—are like precious ore mined from its source. The miner is the writer; the mine is the interview.

In all the art and craft of nonfiction writing, nothing is more important than the interview. As it goes, usually, so goes the piece. Poor interview, poor piece. Good interview, good piece.

Unfortunately, there are no sure-fire procedures, techniques, or gimmicks that will guarantee success. Interviewing always involves at least two people—interviewer and interview subject—and even though the interviewer may do everything right, the interview subject may do everything wrong, and there goes the interview. That's worth remembering. Young writers especially might come out of the mine empty-handed or with low-grade ore, wondering how they'll ever make a piece from such meager material and blaming themselves for not having got more or better from the interview subject. Often, of course, the writer will have been at fault. But no matter how skillful he or she becomes at interviewing, there will always be some interview subject who during the interview becomes a great stone face or unstoppable spieler or undecipherable obfuscator who simply will not yield good material.

Writers must recognize that some people are just poor interviews and there is nothing that can be done to achieve a good result with them. Don't blame yourself and injure your confidence—a valuable asset to an interviewer—unless you're certain you really were the one at fault. On the other hand, realize that not all interviews turn out poorly, and if you've had a string of poor ones, it's probably an indication you're doing something wrong.

An interview, particularly one done on short notice, can be a crap shoot. You just roll—go through the necessary motions—and take your chances. However, skilled interviewers, like smart players, know there are some things they can do to lessen the likelihood of failure and enhance the chance to success. At each of the three stages of an interview a writer can improve his chances of success by following procedures that have proved effective for other successful interviewers.

Arranging the Interview

Some features, usually sidebars to main news stories, grow out of impromptu interviews done on the spot where the news occurs. Such stories often result in little more than a string of quotes and the writer's own observations.

In most cases, however, interviews are set up beforehand. Since the interview subject must consent to an interview and be available for a certain amount of time at a time and place convenient to both the subject and the interviewer, arrangements need to be made in advance. Thus, making the arrangements is the first stage of the interview itself. It requires making contact with either the subject or his representative, a fundamental and obvious, but not always simple, task.

For example, you're working in a city where the one outstanding high school football player, intensely recruited by colleges all over the country, signs a letter of intent to go to the University of Oklahoma, and you decide to go after a story on Oklahoma's recruiting program, focusing on its head football coach. You will need to interview the coach, not just talk on the phone, but meet him, observe him in his natural habitat with his players, get in a conversation with him, watch him react, get the feeling you know him. Only then will you be able to show him to the reader so the reader will get to know him too.

But how do you get the interview?

Perhaps Chrysler Corporation has acquired 5,000 acres near your city to build a revolutionary, computerized manufacturing facility to produce cars of the twenty-first century. You suggest a piece on the man behind this significant development and your editor says, "Let's do it." The man you need to see is chairman of the Chrysler Corporation. What do you do to arrange an interview with him?

It can be tough enough when you know who it is you need to interview; you have his name and some idea of where you can reach him. It's a lot tougher when you don't.

For example, you get an assignment to do a piece on a construction worker, one who works 20 or 30 stories high, assembling the steel framework of a towering new office building. You don't know whom, among the hundreds of such workers, to write about. You have to find one who is reasonably articulate, who is fairly representative of such workers, who has been on the job long enough to have had some interesting experiences to tell about, and who is willing to give you an interview. How do you find him?

In some cases you may have the subject's name but little else. A newspaper in your city publishes a United Press International story datelined McMurdo Sound, Antarctica, with a byline and a precede saying the writer is chief of the Honolulu UPI bureau and that the story was filed on a reporting tour of the South Pacific. The story tells how a young helicopter pilot, a Lt. William Davis, of Charlotte, North Carolina, and two passengers on his helicopter were rescued after three days without food, heat, or radio, in blizzard conditions on an Antarctic ice floe, where their helicopter had been forced down by engine trouble.

Your idea is to do an interview with Davis and write a first-person piece in which he recreates the agonizing hours, the fear, the struggle to stay alive, with details of the whole adventure. You query a national magazine and get a go-ahead on the story. Now, how do you find Davis and arrange an interview?

In virtually every case, you should try to reach your interview subject by telephone. Usually you can be more persuasive on the phone than in a letter or telegram, answering your subject's questions, assuaging his fears, and overcoming his initial reluctance. Also, whether he agrees to the interview or refuses, you'll know immediately, instead of having to wait for days while letters crawl through the postal system.

In any event, no writer should ever feel that someone is unapproachable or unavailable for an interview. When seeking an interview, no matter how important, busy, or remote the person is, you must never assume it can't be done; *never assume a "no" answer.* If you want an interview, ask for it. If the intended interview subject doesn't want to give it to you, make him say no.

Sometimes his "no" answer will take the form of no answer. That is, he will not be reachable and will not return your call. You can write him, send him telegrams asking him to call you collect at his convenience – and still he won't respond. After repeated attempts, realize it's not going to work out and tell your editor.

Ordinarily, it does no good to try to force your way into an interview. Interview subjects who do not want to be interviewed always prove uncooperative and do not yield the ore you need to produce a good piece. A news story doesn't require a cooperative interview subject; his refusal or lack of cooperation is itself a fact of the story and can be reported to the reader. However, a newspaper feature or a magazine article usually requires the cooperation, a willingness to be interviewed, of the interview subject.

Generally if the person sought for the interview is a celebrity or other

VIP, such as the Oklahoma coach and the Chrysler chairman, the writer has a choice of two approaches: direct and indirect.

In the *direct approach*, the writer tries to reach the subject personally, not through a representative (the indirect approach). Thus the first thing that is needed is a phone number where the subject can be reached.

The company, institution, or organization the subject is associated with is usually the best place to start. The coach could be reached through the University of Oklahoma; the chairman through the Chrysler Corporation, for example. Their phone numbers are available from the telephone company information operator once you know the city where the company, institution, or organization is located. If you don't know the city, there is usually some directory that will list the company, institution, or organization and give its address and telephone number, along with other information about it. There is a directory for practically every form of organized human activity, available at any good library. To find out what they are, where they are, and how to use them, simply ask the librarian. (Learn to use and appreciate librarians and their resources.)

Once you have the number, call it. When someone at the other end answers, it's either the person you want, or it's not. If it is, begin stating your business. If it's not, simply ask each new voice for the person you want until you are connected. If you are finally told you can't reach that person, it's probably for one of two reasons.

1. The person you want is ordinarily reachable at this phone but isn't now (because he's "out of town," "in conference," "at lunch," "on another phone," "on vacation," "sick," "at his aunt's funeral," "in the rest room," or otherwise unable to speak on this phone). Once you're told that, you can decide on your next move.

If he isn't available now, you need to find out when he will be available, so you can call back then. Or, depending on the circumstances, you will need to find out how he can be reached now—at another number in the building, in another city, at home, or whatever. When it's important to make arrangements right away, or at least soon, be sure you find out whether the person you want is reachable somewhere else—and if so, how.

Ordinarily, it's not enough merely to leave word you called and ask to have your call returned. You can do it; there's no harm in it. And you might get the call, even long distance. But don't depend on it.

2. Even if you have the right telephone extension, your subject may not be reachable. It's a fact of life that not everyone, especially celebrities and other VIPs, is willing to talk to a stranger, which is what you are. For whatever reason, and often it is legitimate and understandable, some people with whom you seek an interview will not be available through the direct approach. They are reachable only through someone else.

The *indirect approach* works best then, as you might expect it to with the coach and the Chrysler chairman. In some cases, even though the direct method might work, you might want to use the indirect approach anyway. A third person, particularly one who is public-relations conscious, might smooth the path for you. For example, if the Oklahoma coach doesn't really want to do the interview, someone in the OU athletic publicity office might talk him into doing it anyway, pointing out how favorable publicity could help make future recruiting in your city more effective. Or Chrysler's p.r. department might overcome the chairman's reluctance to spend an hour in an interview in which p.r. people see value but the chairman does not.

The indirect approach is likely to mean dealing first or perhaps entirely with one or more of the following:

1. A secretary or administrative assistant, especially one who has the authority to make an appointment for his or her boss, the person you want to interview.

2. An agent, manager, or p.r. representative. This person might be the employee of the person you want to interview, or the person you want to interview might be a client of this person. The approach is the same in either case.

3. Someone in a corporate or institutional public relations department. It might be the p.r. department of the interview subject's company (Chrysler, for example), or a network p.r. department (in the case of a TV entertainer), or a studio p.r. department (in the case of a movie actor or actress), a book publisher's p.r. department (in the case of someone who has written a book, especially one that has been recently published), or the p.r. department of a sports team, such as the Dallas Cowboys or New York Yankees (in the case of a professional football or baseball player), the public affairs department of a branch or unit of the military services, or the publicity agent (often uncomplimentarily called a "flack" by writers and editors) for the celebrity you want to interview or for the local sponsor of the celebrity who is coming to your city to give a concert, show, speech, or some other kind of performance.

People in p.r. departments are generally of great service to writers seeking an interview. Putting their client, employer, or employee in touch with representatives of communications media is part of their job. Journalistic ethics and your own personal integrity usually dictate that you neither give nor receive any compensation for the interview. You are paid by your publication—either as a freelance or staffer—and the p.r. representative is paid by his client or employer. No other compensation should be promised or made.

Although the indirect approach can often prove the smoothest way to the interview subject, you should not be timid about using the direct approach, which has at least two advantages: It's quicker, so you usually get an answer to your request for an interview immediately; and it breaks the ice, so when you go to the interview, you've already introduced yourself on the phone and held a conversation with the subject. Usually the more challenging problem is not whether to choose the direct or indirect approach, but rather how to find the person you need to interview. Resourcefulness and determination are often required, along with luck.

Not long ago, I got an assignment from *D Magazine,* the city magazine in Dallas, to do an article on leisure homes. The piece was to show the reader three examples of leisure homes and their owners. One was to be a cabin-in-the-woods sort of retreat; one was to be a cottage at a lake; and the third was to be a home in a golf-and-country-club development.

A newcomer to the Dallas area, I had not one such place in mind and knew no one who owned a leisure home. But on the day after I got the assignment, I happened to have my first appointment with a dentist in the community near Dallas where I lived. In the course of getting to know each other, the dentist asked me what I did for a living, and I told him I was a magazine writer. "As a matter of fact," I said, "I just got an assignment from *D Magazine* to do a piece on leisure homes." I described to him the places I needed to find.

"My brother," he volunteered, "is building a place like that at Cypress Lake."

"Is that so?" I said. "Do you think he'd mind talking to me about it?"

No, he said, he was sure his brother wouldn't mind, that he would be glad to help.

From that fortuitous conversation, I was led to a string of contacts that resulted in my finding two of the three examples I needed.

Talking to people who can help you is a must in the pursuit of an interview. To find the person you need to interview for the piece on construction workers who are building the new office building in your city, you would have to talk to people who are in a position to know those workers—someone in a management job at the construction company, for example, or an official in the union to which the workers belong. You could go to a bar or restaurant near the construction site, where the workers might gather sometime during the day, and talk to them until you've found the right one. Richard Schneider, a senior editor of *Guideposts* magazine, once did a piece on one such worker. He found his man through the public relations department of the union's headquarters.

To locate the helicopter pilot who survived three days on the stormbound ice floe, you could try several means: Contact the author of the story at the UPI office in Honolulu and ask him where the pilot is now, or where he was last; or contact the pilot's hometown newspaper, the *Charlotte Observer,* to see if they've got more on him and can tell you how to reach him; or contact the Department of Defense public affairs department at the Pentagon and let them find him for you.

Freelance writer Toby Smith got an assignment similar to that one, and he used a combination of contacts. From the author of the UPI story he learned what branch of the military service the pilot was in (since the story identified him merely as Lt. William Davis he could have been in the Army, Navy, Marines, or Air Force) and where he was stationed. Once he had that information, supplied by the UPI Honolulu bureau chief, Smith phoned the Navy base, reached the base locator (the person who can provide phone numbers to reach personnel at that base), and asked for and received information on how to contact Davis.

After you've finally got the right address or phone number and have decided whether the direct or indirect approach is appropriate for the person and the circumstances, you are ready to get the interview.

Paving the Way to a Good Interview

Once the intended interview subject, or his representative, is on the phone, the interviewer's job is to sell the idea of doing the interview. What you, the interviewer, say and how you say it can make the difference between success and failure in your attempt to get the interview. If the initial contact is handled well, it can pave the way to a good interview.

KNOW WHAT YOU'RE GOING TO SAY. You want the interview subject to believe you've got it all under control, and the best way to do that is to be prepared. If necessary, list the information you must give to or get from the interview subject. If you don't write the list down, at least have it firmly in your mind. You will feel a little sheepish and professionally awkward if you forget something and have to call back. And make sure you've got paper and a pencil beside you at the phone.

BE COURTEOUS. The intended interview subject has something you want—his time and cooperation—and you have to ask him for it. Realize you're asking a favor—even if the resulting article or feature works to the advantage of the subject, and be polite in what you say and how you say it. When arranging an interview, the writer becomes a salesman. Persuasion is the appropriate tactic.

INTRODUCE YOURSELF. Open the conversation in the same way you would if you were introducing yourself face to face. Tell the interview subject who you are (give your last name as well as your first) and if possible identify yourself with a publication. The name of a publication will carry of lot more weight than your name will. If the publication is a special interest magazine or paper, obscure to general readers, tell the subject something about it—its audience, its subject matter, its circulation, and so forth. Big circulation numbers or special audience characteristics can be persuasive.

Identifying with a publication is a simple matter for a staff writer ("I'm Joan Wilson of *The New York Times*."). For a freelance, it's a little trickier and requires some knowledge of the way publications, particularly magazines, the biggest users of freelance material, operate.

Not counting staff-written material, written by salaried employees, publications generally acquire most of their material in three ways: by assignment, when a specific piece is assigned to a specific writer and payment of a certain amount is promised, usually upon acceptance of the article by the editors; on speculation, when the publication, usually following a query from the writer, expresses interest in the proposed piece but promises nothing except a careful reading of the finished manuscript, with an eye to buying it if the editors like it; and unsolicited, when a writer writes the piece and sends it to the publication unheralded and unexpected.

If you are working as a freelance on assignment, you can identify yourself with the publication like this: "I'm Joan Wilson and I'm doing an article for *The New York Times Magazine*." You can do the same if you have queried a publication and have been told by an editor that he's willing to see the finished piece on speculation. In that event, you are still doing the piece for a specific publication and with their knowledge.

However, if you are doing the piece on your own, to be submitted unsolicited, you should avoid mentioning the name of a publication. Merely say who you are and what you're doing. If the interview subject asks where the piece is to be published, you can say you're planning to submit it to whatever magazine or paper you think is a possible market for it. But be careful: Don't misrepresent yourself. Doing the piece on your own—as a freelance without an assignment and without an expression of interest from an editor—is a handicap, but far from a fatal, or even a terribly serious, one. As far as arranging the interview is concerned, you simply work without the advantage of a publication behind you.

TELL WHAT YOU WANT FROM THE SUBJECT. Avoid telling the interview subject you want an interview. That's liable to mean different things to different people. Instead, say you want to talk about whatever the article is to be about. Tell the subject what he or she needs to know. For example, say how much time you'll need. Many people you will interview will be those whose time is especially precious. They want to know in advance how much time is involved, so they can plan their day. Any interview subject should know what you expect. Say you'll need "about an hour," or "about an hour and a half." Ordinarily, most interviews for pieces up to 1500 words require no more than an hour and a half. If the intended article is a personality piece of 2500 words or more, you may need two or three days with the subject, and if you do, say so.

Ask if you can meet at a time when he will be undisturbed – by phone calls, kids, secretary, etc. – and relaxed. In some cases, you'll want to observe the subject doing his thing – such as the Oklahoma football coach on the road, recruiting his ballplayers, or the Chrysler chairman on the job, acting in relation to his fellow workers. When such circumstances are needed, say so.

Try to accommodate the subject and his schedule, but say what you need. If you can meet only on certain days, say so. But say it diplomatically. For example, if you are doing a freelance piece and can meet with the interview subject only on a weekend, you could say, "Is it possible to meet with you on a Saturday or maybe a Sunday?" In most cases, the subject will probably be able to accommodate your schedule, but it's usually better to ask for his or her help in solving the problem, rather than dictate the solution.

Interview subjects usually perform best on their own turf. For that reason, it's usually best to go where the subject is, rather than have him or her come to you. Depending on the circumstances and the nature of the piece, the interview should be done where the subject lives (including a hotel suite or a jail cell) or works or otherwise does his or her thing. It might be done both at home and at work. Don't say you want to come to his house; say you need to see him in a place where he'll be comfortable. But be ready to accept second best.

If you know what the angle (see Chapter 5) of your piece is to be, what specific kind of material you need, tell the subject that, too. For example, you may be doing a feature on a United States senator from your state. During an interview there's almost a limitless number of topics you could cover. But the piece you have in mind is a Father's Day feature about how the senator's father was the inspiration to become a successful public official. If you know that's the story you're going after, explain it so the senator will prepared to talk about it. On the other hand, if the piece is to be about the senator's stand on nuclear waste material being stored in your state, say so. When the subject is prepared to talk about the things you want him to, you're more likely to have a good interview.

INQUIRE ABOUT AVAILABLE INFORMATION. In some circumstances, it's a good idea to ask about any previously published material that pertains to the piece you're doing. If the interview is being arranged through a p.r. person, it's especially appropriate to talk to him or her about what you need: reprints or photocopies of other pieces on the subject; press releases; information sheets, including biographical data; brochures, etc. The more you know about the subject before the interview, the better the interview is likely to go. If it seems reasonable that some material may be available only from the subject or his representative (or if it's a lot easier getting it that way than tracking down obscure publications in libraries to photocopy earlier articles), ask for it.

ASK FOR DIRECTIONS AND OTHER SPECIAL INSTRUCTIONS. Sometimes you need to know more than the address of the subject's home or office, or wherever the interview is to be held. You might also need directions to find the house or apartment or office, especially if it's in a city strange to you.

In addition, you might need special instructions to reach the subject. Many office and apartment buildings, for example, have elaborate security systems through which all visitors must pass, so you need to know what to expect and how to cope. Or you may need instructions on where to park you car, which entrance to use, or where you must change elevators. There can be many such things you need to know to save time, anxiety, and possibly embarrassment. Before ending the call say, "Is there anything else I need to know in order to find you?"—or words to that effect.

MAKE SURE THE SUBJECT HAS YOUR NAME AND PHONE NUMBER. In case something happens and the subject cannot keep the interview appointment, he or she will need to know how to contact you. Before you hang up, say something like this: "Let me give you my phone number, just in case something comes up and we have to set a new date." Then give your name again—unless you're sure she knows it—and your phone number.

SAY THANK YOU. Remember, you've been given something worthwhile, so don't forget to express your appreciation.

Preparing for the Interview

It's not enough for the interviewer to arrange the interview, then show up at the appointed place and hour with only a quick mind and glib tongue. Mental agility and conversational ability are necessary, but they're not everything. If you've got time to prepare for the interview, prepare. It's the best way. Don't wing it unless you have to. Only a desperate lack of time—when your editor gives you the assignment with no advance notice and demands copy within a couple of hours, for example—should keep you from careful preparation. There are several steps in the preparation stage.

FIND OUT AS MUCH AS POSSIBLE ABOUT THE SUBJECT. What makes him worth writing and reading about? If possible, check the local newspaper's morgue file. Also check the *Reader's Guide to Periodical Literature*—and any other index you think might indicate if a national or regional magazine has done a piece on him. Make photocopies of all the stories and articles you find. Gather whatever material is available, including whatever you can get from the subject or his representative and read it all. Don't waste interview time—and risk offending the subject as well—by asking for information you could have got earlier.

DECIDE WHAT THE PIECE MUST INCLUDE. This step is one of the most important, helpful, and economical. Ideally, you should visualize the article, or better yet put it in outline form on paper, before going to the interview. Doing so can be an immense advantage once the interview starts. You will know precisely the information—or the *kinds* of information—you must gather to make a good, thorough, and readable piece. You'll know exactly what to look for in the interview, go straight to it, and make sure you've got everything before you leave—thus avoiding an expensive (perhaps) and embarrassing (probably) second interview. You'll know what isn't necessary, too, and not waste time collecting it; you'll also know when to stop the interview.

For example, let's say you're going to do the piece on the University of Oklahoma's football recruiting program. Think about that a few minutes.

What should the piece include? You want the reader to see how OU recruits great players. So you need information to let the reader see how the recruiting program works: how names of high school players are fed into the screening system; who submits names, what information about the players is included, how the information is processed, how it is used, who does what with it. Write down the pieces of information you will need. Don't be afraid to include too much at this stage. Plan to get more—as long as it is pertinent to the planned piece—than you'll be able to use. Better to have it and not need it, than need it and not have it.

Now, what else should the piece include? Well, since Oklahoma coaches seem consistently successful recruiters, you probably ought to include information that will document their success and show the reader that the program works.

Also, assuming the head coach is the key figure in the recruiting program, you will need to show the kind of person he is, how he works with assistant coaches and alumni, and how he operates with recruits and their parents. And you'll probably want some personal background and family information. Maybe you'll want to include what other coaches say about the University of Oklahoma's recruitment program. Maybe you'll want to talk to some recently recruited players and their parents, to see the recruiting program from the players' and parents' perspectives so the reader will be able to see them, too.

Write down all of that, listing those items of information you'll need. Don't take shortcuts, avoiding bothersome steps of preparation, unless forced to by the exigencies of the deadline.

By now you've already got a picture of how the piece is to go, just from thinking about it as much as you have. Later you will refine it, creating categories of information and arranging them in a logical sequence for the reader.

Also by now you have discovered which people you need to interview for the piece and what specific information you need from them. You know what you're going after.

Or maybe that's not the piece you have in mind. Maybe it includes too much and takes too much time and money to report. Maybe instead the piece should be about the head coach, focused on his recruiting. If the piece is on the coach himself, it becomes a simpler piece to do. All you really need is one source—the coach himself. Show the coach doing his recruiting thing, show him in relation to other people, and let the reader get to know him as a person, by getting to know something of him as a person yourself. That's done through an interview.

In either case, by thinking the piece through, by considering it from different approaches, you can decide the best course to follow. You will see the piece in your head—then be prepared to go to the interview (or interviews) to mine the ore.

GET A TAPE RECORDER, TAPES, AND BATTERIES. From centuries of man's inventiveness have come two great devices to ease the writer's burden: the typewriter and the tape recorder. Of the two, there is no question that the tape recorder is the bigger boon. And if ever forced to choose between them, like a man serving two masters, it would be the tape recorder I'd prefer, and the typewriter I'd not.

If you have never used a tape recorder for interviews, do so now. A good tape recorder will create a faithful, verbatim reproduction of the interview, not merely the words spoken by you and the interview subject, but a complete aural record of the event, capable of being replayed repeatedly, including tone of voice, significant pauses, laughter, everything, just the way it occurred. With a tape recorder you, the interviewer, can concentrate on the interview subject instead of on note-taking, letting you maintain eye contact, letting the subject know you're listening, letting you, in short, carry on a conversation rather than an inquiry. Moreover a recorder provides a timing device, signaling the end of the tape so you avoid the distracting glances at your wristwatch to check the time – a real conversation-killer.

As with any other piece of machinery, things can go wrong with a tape recorder. A few precautions, however, will minimize the risk. For example, it's best to buy fresh batteries, the standard rather than the everlasting kind, for each interview and then discard them when it's over. That way, you can be sure the batteries won't run out, without having to keep track of when you bought them or how many hours you've used them (you don't want to be a bookkeeper instead of a writer). Fresh batteries and new tapes are a lot cheaper than airplane tickets, car rentals, hotel and meal bills. There's no point in gambling on three dollars' worth of batteries when all the expense of the interview, plus the article itself, is at stake. Get new batteries, get new tapes.

Test your batteries and tapes in your recorder before you leave for the interview to be sure all are working. It's also a good idea to record a few seconds of music from a radio or record onto the tape. That way, if during the interview you forget to depress the "record" button, the music will start to play and you'll realize your oversight. Otherwise, you might come back with a blank tape.

Using a tape recorder is a lot like placing all your eggs in one basket. When it works, you have the interview securely contained on tape, but if the recorder or the cassette malfunctions, you may have a blank or garbled tape. If such a disaster strikes, you must as soon as possible, within a couple of hours, get to a typewriter and type everything you can remember.

ASSEMBLE ALL MATERIALS. Take with you: the tape recorder, ready to go; spare tapes, batteries, or a plug-in cord if your recorder is AC/DC (just in case); pencils or ballpoint pens (at least two); paper; the list of information you decided you must gather for the piece; directions and instructions to find the subject; and other material you might want to refer to or ask the subject about. All those materials can be contained in an attaché case or shoulder bag so you have only one item to carry. An attaché is preferable because when placed on your lap or beside you on a couch, it provides a writing surface – which you may need because there will be *some* things on which you'll want to take notes.

PSYCH YOURSELF. Don't underestimate the value of mental preparation for the interview. Even experienced interviewers sometimes feel put off by the subject, because he or she is a very important person. You are not immune. Depending on (a) who it is you're going to interview and (b) where you are in your development as an interviewer, you too will occasionally feel a little intimidated, especially early in your career, more especially if you happen to be somewhat shy.

Some anxiety is good; it pumps up your adrenalin and puts you on your toes. But high anxiety, brought on by feelings of inadequacy and fear of failure, works against you, diminishing your chances for a successful interview. Under stress, your mind fails to function at its best. You will have difficulty achieving the naturalness and openness that a good interview requires.

On the way to the interview, remind yourself that you are reasonably bright and articulate and that you can hold your own in a conversation, particularly one in which you are more listener than talker (which is what you must be in the interview). Remind yourself also that what you do as a writer—communicating information to mass audiences—is, in the overall scheme of things, just as important as what the subject does. Our society assigns roles to its members, just as nature does, and the whole functions properly only when individual members do their parts. Your part is to provide information—interestingly, accurately, clearly—and it's an immensely important job, vital to our society.

If you have prepared for the interview, you'll look forward to it eagerly rather than dreading it. If, on the other hand, you see the interview as something to be endured and are hardly able to wait until it's over and you're back in your car, you probably will have a poor interview—and a poor piece.

Develop enthusiasm for the story you're about to get from your subject. Go to the interview expecting a good story, believing you will appear confident and professional. Go believing you will enjoy the experience. Go knowing you are as prepared as you can be.

Interviewing the Subject

Interviews generally come in two varieties, and the interviewer must choose one or both, depending on the requirements of the piece. One kind is the *action interview*, in which the information gathered is acted out by the subject, usually in situations involving other people, while the interviewer accompanies the subject (sometimes at a distance, unobtrusively) and is a witness to whatever occurs. For example, when you, the interviewer, go with the football coach onto the field or into the locker room where there are players and other coaches and observe him doing what a head coach does, it's an action interview. The things he says and does can then be recreated in scenes in the piece you write – so the reader may in effect stand in your shoes, seeing, hearing, smelling the same things you did during the interview. Many pieces are done just that way.

Here's an excerpt from an article by Paula Wallace Streeter about a dog catcher, whom she interviewed while he was on the job. It's an example of the kind of material gained from an action interview:

The dispatcher called Gene on a loose-dog complaint: A dog in the northwest section was getting into garbage.

Gene spotted the animal soon after entering the area and followed it for a block before finding out who the owner was. A neighbor identified the dog. Gene stopped at the owner's house.

While Gene wrote out the citation for letting an animal roam loose, the woman swore her dog hadn't been running loose. Gene continued writing, explaining he had chased the animal. What if her dog had been hit by a car? he asked.

The woman walked inside. When she reappeared, Gene stopped writing.

She was carrying a rifle.

Her dog didn't get into other people's garbage, she said, and no dog catcher was going to take it or write her a ticket!

Gene radioed for a backup, a police unit, then tried to talk with the woman and her husband. She had received a warning before, he told her. Her husband had been warned about allowing the dog to run loose. She denied it.

If her husband didn't agree with him, Gene said, he would rip up the citation and forget the incident.

The husband denied being warned.

Gene ripped out the citation and put his pen away. The next time he caught their dog, he said, he was going to write a citation for every infraction possible, not because he had lost his gambit, but because they had lied to him.

The following example of the action interview is an excerpt from a profile of photographer Joel Meyerowitz, by Gerald Peary, published in *Boston* magazine:

On a clear, warm late-summer afternoon, Joel Meyerowitz and family (his sculptor wife, Vivian Bower; his son, Sasha, 15; his daughter, Ariel, 12) drive out to Ballston Beach, in nearby Truro, site of some memorable *Cape Light* photographs. Meyerowitz sets up his tripod in the sand and goes for a swim in the cold Atlantic. Refreshed, he picks up the Deardorff and tripod and wanders down the beach, eyes wide open.

"There's something about a fleshy person against the sunlight," Meyerowitz has said. "Flesh and sun and water – that's how it all began."

Everybody on Ballston Beach knows him or has heard about him. "Hi Joel!" sunbathers call out frequently. A man walks up and says, "I want to tell you how much your pictures have meant to me. I live in that house up there. If you ever need a glass of water, stop by."

Meyerowitz is polite, but continues taking in the water and studying people on their beach towels. Thinking photography, he is getting a faraway look.

"When I walk along the beach and come face-to-face with a photograph, sometimes I know right away," he tells me, as we stroll in the sand. "Just as often a picture grows on me. Being on the beach is not about waiting for the light to get better. It's waiting for myself to fill up, to get that tingle all over."

Like a hyper-romantic Method actor, Meyerowitz must feel certain things inside before he can photograph, especially when he is shooting people. "I want them to sense something unusual," he explains, "my intensity, my behavior. When I shoot, there is an element of hypnosis, akin to the whispering seduction of fashion photographers. When I look with excitation, I *really* see, and people may reveal more. It's the harmony and beauty of the dance that's the ideal result."

Suddenly, on Ballston Beach, the picture is there. A woman in a red bathing suit and a yellow bathing cap is swimming up and down the surf. Meyerowitz stops talking and smiles, almost half-madly, to himself.

For 10 minutes he watches this for-

tyish woman swim, enjoying her confident strokes – Meyerowitz was a champion swimmer at Ohio State University – and drinking in the red and yellow colors plunked in the blue, blue sea. "I'm allowing myself to be mesmerized," he says, "until I'm committed."

When the woman comes out of the water, he boldly walks up and asks to take her picture. The woman says yes and, dripping water, she looks smack into the camera for her portrait. "She didn't play any games. She allowed herself to be calm," Meyerowitz says afterward, with admiration. "A woman confronting her destiny" is how he labels such a photographic encounter.

The other kind is the *static interview*. In it the information gathered comes mostly from the subject's memory, not from what he does during the interview. The static interview, which can cover the entire range of the subject's experience and knowledge, is by far the more common type. Even when, as in the excerpted dog catcher and photographer articles, there is information to be drawn from both kinds of interviews, much will come from the static interview. It is, in essence, merely a conversation between the interviewer and the interview subject, but one in which the interviewer chooses the topics and the degree of detail in which the topics are discussed.

The following guides to successful interviewing pertain to the static interview. Most pertain to the action interview as well.

ACHIEVE THE RIGHT CONDITIONS. On the phone, you told the subject or his representative what you needed. Now try your best to get it. If it's an action interview, go with the subject while he does his thing, as arranged. If it's a static interview, talk to him in a place where he is relaxed, uninhibited, and uninterrupted. You're going to be at it for more than an hour; try to steer him or her to a room where both of you will be comfortable.

Avoid third parties in the room with you. The interview will go best with just the two of you – unless, of course, someone else is needed as a source. Others in the room may exert an inhibiting influence on the subject, preventing the openness and intimacy you need. Especially try to exclude public relations people from the interview if at all possible. They are among the worst inhibitors.

(The least satisfactory interview conditions I can remember occurred in an interview with a woman astronaut, held, of all places, in the p.r. person's office, where I sat facing the astronaut while the p.r. person sat behind me, also facing the astronaut. Throughout the interview I felt the p.r. person was flashing signals behind my back to the astronaut as she responded to my questions. A similarly poor situation occurred in an interview with a Red Chinese defector, held in a Washington, D.C., hotel room with a U.S. State Department p.r. person sitting in with us, obviously monitoring the interview. At one point he interrupted the conversation and asked me to shut off the tape recorder because he thought the subject was about to reveal too much. Neither piece worked out.)

It's good to have other people around, though not in the same room. If someone else is in the house or office, the subject doesn't have to bother answering doorbells and telephones, or attend to small children. If during the phone contact you told the subject or his representative you needed a place where the subject would be relatively uninterrupted, or if the subject is a veteran at being interviewed, you should have no problem. One year I interviewed both Ron Guidry, the New York Yankee pitcher, and Ken Forsch, then a pitcher for the Houston Astros, in their homes. Both had young daughters. Both managed to have the children at someone else's house on the day of the interview. The Guidrys, however, had a problem in their bathroom that morning, and Ron was up and down with the plumber during the interview.

Try to place the tape recorder where it will be relatively inconspicuous and will not pick up interfering background noises. I once interviewed a New Jersey couple who perceived the interview as a social occasion and, shortly after I arrived, graciously sat me down to an elaborate lunch at the kitchen table, on which I had to place my tape recorder so the interview could continue while we ate. When the interview was over and I played the tape back, much of what was on it was the sounds of bowls bumping, knives scraping, dishes clattering, glasses clinking.

PUT THE SUBJECT AT EASE. Sometimes the subject will feel intimidated by you. Not all interview subjects are sophisticated and socially adept, and those who have not been interviewed before may feel apprehensive about it, not knowing what to expect. It's your job to put the subject at ease and help him be his natural self, which he must be if the interview is to succeed. Ordinarily the best way to relax the subject is to be relaxed and natural yourself. Be friendly, courteous, warm.

Turn on the tape recorder while you're still making small talk, perhaps deliberately calling attention to the recorder, saying offhand, "The tape recorder won't bother you, will it?" He'll usually say, "No," realizing he shouldn't be bothered by it. After that, ignore the recorder till it signals it's time to turn the cassette over. Try to keep the subject's mind off the recorder and on the conversation. One possible bad effect of recorders is what can be called "the wary wording reaction." When that happens, the subject becomes extremely guarded in responding, sometimes answering precisely but sounding stilted and perhaps even silly — the way police officials often sound speaking into a TV camera. Another effect can be called "the speechifying reaction." Some subjects, noticing the tape recorder, believe they are delivering messages meant for posterity. They shift into their oratorical mode when the taped conversation begins.

Usually the subject is more likely to forget the recorder than you are. You might want to check it occasionally, but don't let the subject think something's wrong. Do it unobtrusively, saying, "Tape recorders are a big advantage over note-taking, but I *do* worry about them sometimes." Then immediately resume the conversation.

Don't be afraid to spend a few minutes talking about the weather or whether you had trouble finding the place, or anything else that has nothing to do with the information you need. Let the tape recorder run. Concentrate on trying to establish an easy, open feeling; then move into the substantive part of the interview once you and the subject have felt each other out and are comfortable. It is time well spent if it loosens you both up.

ESTABLISH A CONVERSATION. Talk; don't interrogate. Refer to your list of items to cover. Bring them up in conversation, not necessarily by asking questions. Instead of asking, "How did you feel when he pointed the gun at you?" you can say, "I've wondered what it must be like to have a pistol aimed right at you," then stop and let the subject tell you. By so doing, you'll encourage him to volunteer information. His responses won't be limited to mere answers to your questions. You'll avoid having him lie back, once an answer is given, waiting for the next question, like a batter waiting for the next pitch.

The rules for being a good conversationalist apply to the interviewer. You must be a good listener and you must show interest. Most people like to talk about themselves and what they're interested in, so make that work to your advantage. Show the subject you are interested in what he has to say. Draw him out.

ASK THOUGHTFUL QUESTIONS. Avoid questions that call for a "yes" or "no" answer. Avoid letting the subject give you an answer shorter than your question. Encourage him to elaborate, go into detail, and explain when necessary.

GUIDE THE INTERVIEW. Beware of two dangers. One is the tendency to put too much of yourself into the conversation, phrasing and rephrasing questions, supplying answers yourself when you see the subject hesitating. You must let the subject do the talking. During moments of awkward silence, don't rush in to fill the void of wordlessness yourself; wait for the subject to be first to relieve the discomfort of silence by speaking again. Remember that it's what the interview subject has to say, not the interviewer, that's important. Your job as interviewer is to turn on the lights, not to glow yourself.

The other danger is that the interview subject will become a runaway automobile, taking off out of control, unstoppable, unsteerable. The resulting wreckage, that hulk at the bottom of the hill, is your article. Good luck on selling that mess!

The trick is to let the subject do the talking, but guide the conversation to the things you want him to talk about. Politely interrupt him if he strays too far; bring him back to the information you need. You're in charge of the interview, and if you're not, you're in trouble—and so is the article.

MAKE THE SUBJECT TELL STORIES. To write a good piece, you're going to need anecdotes—great, precious nuggets. Don't come out of the mine without them. Encourage the interview subject to tell stories about himself, and about people connected with him.

When you write the piece, you will have to let the reader see the subject in action, not simply talking. So you must, in conversation with him, draw out his experiences. For the piece about the Oklahoma football coach, you must get specific cases of recruiting from him—actual experiences he has had with specific players and their parents and high school coaches, experiences that can let the reader see the coach in action.

There are only two ways to get anecdotes: (a) witness the action yourself or (b) get an account of it from someone else. In most cases, you will have no choice; you must get it from someone else. Good anecdotal material is the nonfiction writer's key to success, whether the medium is newspaper features, magazine articles, or books.

Encourage the subject to relate specific incidents that have formed his opinions. "Maine is a great place to take a vacation," he might say, for example. Then you say something to force him to recall—and describe—a specific experience that illustrates and supports his generalization. If he has difficulty remembering a specific experience, ask about the first time (the first time a person does anything is usually memorable) or the last time. "Tell me about a really good vacation you had in Maine," you might say. And he's likely to answer, "Oh, there've been a lot of 'em." Then press again for a specific. "Tell me about the first time you remember taking a vacation in Maine. How long ago was it?"

Something that usually will *not* work is a request for an anecdote. "I need an anecdote. Can you give me an anecdote about vacationing in Maine?" The subject will probably have no clear idea of what you're talking about. Don't be timid about volunteering information about yourself, telling an anecdote of your own, as you would in normal conversation, as a pump-priming device, encouraging him to respond by recounting *his* experience.

Interviews for pieces written as continuous narrative – for example, the Antarctic helicopter pilot's story – are much simpler to conduct than those in which the interviewer has to fish for a collection of anecdotes that will provide the backbone of the piece. The continuous narrative piece tells, in effect, one long anecdote with different scenes. Therefore, in the interview, you need only have the subject recount what happened from the beginning to the conclusion of the action. Your main question in that sort of interview will be simply, "And then what happened?" or "What did you do next?"

Don't forget that when you write the piece, you will have to reconstruct dialogue, letting the characters speak. So you must get the subject to tell you, as part of the story he's recounting, what was said and what he thought while the action was occurring. For example, a spelunker might say in the interview, "By then, I was so turned around, and it was so dark in the cave, I was praying I'd be able to find my way out." If you ask, "Were you actually praying? What exactly did you say?," he's likely to tell you, "Oh, I don't remember – something like, 'God, please don't let me die in this place. Help me find the way out.' "

Get the quotes. Find out what the subject said and what the other person said.

DRAW OUT DESCRIPTION AND OTHER SPECIFIC DETAILS. When you write the piece, you must *show* scenes, characters, objects. To do so, you must envision the scene and the characters clearly yourself. You must get that picture from the interview subject's description (unless, of course, you were a witness to it yourself). Ask for specifics such as names, dates, days of the week, times, people's ages, physical description, quantities, amounts, numbers, colors, locations, directions, job titles, breeds of dogs, or kinds of trees – specifics, specifics, specifics. The more specifics, the better you can recreate and document the event; the better the reader can see it; and the more authentic and believable the piece will be.

PURSUE POSSIBLE ANGLES. The piece is going to need an angle. For example, the piece about the Chrysler chairman is not intended to be an article *all* about him, a biography, but rather to focus on him in relation to the new manufacturing facility Chrysler is planning for your city. During the interview, you would go after the material needed to write *that* piece. However, if for some reason you don't know what the angle of the piece is to be, talk with the subject about a variety of things in his life until he reveals a possible angle, often through anecdotes he tells, then settle on that aspect and have him elaborate on it.

For example, to do the piece about the construction worker on the high-rise office building, you might go into the interview knowing generally it's to be a piece about the worker and what he does, but you don't know exactly what the piece will be about. You probably will not know until you've talked with the worker awhile and heard about some of his experiences, feelings, and worries about a potentially dangerous job, and about a typical day. If he reveals good material about how his wife feels about it, how she lives in fear of an accident, how a fall once did affect their lives, then you might decide to build the entire piece around that aspect of the man and his work. Or if it turns out that he sees his job pretty much the way an office worker sees his – starting at 8 A.M., doing the same old thing, breaking for lunch, going back to the routine, knocking off at 4:30 – then you might build the piece around that idea.

If you don't know exactly what you're going after, you'll need to fish a bit. The trick is to know when you've got a possible angle on the line, then carefully make the catch.

There will be times when you have some idea of the angle, but as the interview gets started, you discover it won't work. It could be because you – or your editor – made a wrong assumption, or you got bad information, or maybe the interview subject just doesn't want to talk about it.

Before going to my interview with Ken Forsch, I had decided on an angle but had not mentioned it to Ken on the phone. In the previous season, both Ken and his brother Bob, a pitcher for the St. Louis Cardinals, had pitched no-hit games, the only brothers in major league baseball to pitch no-hitters the same year – a great curiosity. I had pointed out the curiosity to my editor and said the piece ought to be about brothers – sibling rivalry, family togetherness, growing up with a brother who does the same things you do. The exact focus would come out of the interview, but it would capitalize on the oddity of the brothers' no-hitters. When the interview started, however, I discovered Ken didn't want to talk about what I wanted him to talk about. My early, leading questions were deflected with a polite but firm response: "You'll have to ask Bob about that." The interview moved to other topics, becoming a fishing expedition as I sought some other possible angle and eventually found one.

Go into the interview prepared to shift topics if necessary. Minimize the dangers of surprise by being prepared to adjust to unexpected responses.

MAKE NOTES ON ITEMS TO BE RETURNED TO. While the subject is talking, he may mention something or you may think of something you want to ask about. If so, jot it down. Avoid interrupting, especially if he's telling an anecdote, so that you don't dispel the mood or sidetrack him from what he intended to tell you. Write down what you want to ask about, then come back to it at a stopping place in the conversation.

KNOW WHEN TO QUIT. If you promised that the interview would take a specified amount of time, keep your promise. If you said "about an hour," take the hour, but don't take much more. The subject probably won't mind another 10 or 15 minutes, but don't take liberties; you might have to go back to him later. When the recorder signals the one-hour tape has ended, you've got 15 to 20 minutes left to wrap up the interview—unless the subject has *clearly* signalled that more time is okay (by offering enthusiastically to take you on a tour of the building or the grounds, for example).

BE AN OBSERVER AS WELL AS A LISTENER. Take note of the surroundings and the physical appearance and mannerisms of the subject. The subject's preference in cars, home or office decor, clothing, etc., can reveal a great deal about the person. Even if some such details aren't particularly significant, they at least allow the reader to see the subject more clearly.

EXPRESS GRATITUDE. Thank the subject for the interview. He's given you his time and cooperation; let him know you're grateful.

LEAVE THE DOOR OPEN FOR A FOLLOW-UP. There's always a chance you will need more information and you will avoid embarrassment if you have already suggested that you might phone again. You could say, "When I sit down to my typewriter, I might remember something I forgot to ask you. May I give you a phone call if that happens?" The subject will always agree and you will have prepared him for another contact. There will be no surprise if you do call for more material or to check some piece of information with him.

The GOSS Method of Interviewing

Going into an interview knowing what the angle is, or might be, is the best way. However, optimum conditions don't always prevail. In many cases, you won't know, particularly it you're a newspaper staffer working on short deadlines, without time to adequately research and mull over the assignment. Often you will go to the interview knowing little more than the subject's name and the time and place of the interview. You will have to go in cold turkey—no angle, no list of topic areas or questions, no preparation except the most meager kind.

When that happens, is there any way to save you from humiliation and abject failure?

Yes. There is a formula that can be applied to virtually all interviews meant to result in a feature or article about a person (a piece usually called a *profile*). The formula may also be applied in cases where the expected piece can be reported from one source. This formula provides a universal set of questions to ask a subject. Although there are several such formulas, the simplest and easiest to remember is the GOSS formula, developed by LaRue Gilleland, a University of Nevada journalism professor. It has nothing to do with Goss, a company that manufactures printing equipment, but the similarity in names makes the formula easier to remember. GOSS is an acronym formed from the following words: Goal, Obstacle, Solution, Start.

Nearly everyone (as well as nearly every company, institution, and organization, all of which are represented by people who can be interviewed) has, or in the past has had, a goal of some sort— a dream, an ambition, a purpose, or a reason for being. That goal may lie at the heart of your interview subject's interest, and most people are willing to talk about the things that interest them. Therefore, the idea is for you to get the subject to talk about his *goal*. It might be something as grand as what he hopes to accomplish in life, or perhaps no grander than his purpose in making the movie he made, writing the book he wrote, opening his new store, building a model airplane, or whatever interesting thing he did.

If there is a goal, the subject has either reached it or he hasn't. If he has not reached it, there is probably some obstacle—maybe more than one—that stands in his way and must be overcome, removed, or circumvented if he is to reach his goal. Or if he has already reached the goal, there probably was an obstacle that had to be overcome, removed, or circumvented. Ask him to tell you about the *obstacle* to success.

If the goal has not been reached and the obstacle is still in the way, find out what the subject must do, or what he plans to do, to get around it, over it, or remove it. Find out the *solution*. If the goal has already been reached, ask him what the solution was and how he found it and applied it.

The final step is to ask about the *start* of the idea or project: when and how he happened to get involved. Talk to him about the *start* of the formation of his goal.

There is one other aspect you should ask about: the future. Find out what's going to happen next, what's the next thing he intends to do.

Chances are if you ask the subject what his goal is, you won't get a usable answer. Phrase the question in down-to-earth terms. Here are some specific questions you might ask in each of the GOSS sections. Ask them in a normal, getting-acquainted sort of conversation:

G – "What are you trying to accomplish?"
"What's the purpose of your organization?"
"What do you really want to do?"
"If you could do just one big thing with your life, what would it be?"

O – "What's standing in your way?"
"What problems did you face?"
"Why couldn't you do it?"
"Why don't you do it?"

S – "What are you going to do about it?"
"How did you handle the problem?"
"Is there some way to resolve it?"
"How did you manage it?"

S – "When did the program get started?"
"Whose idea was it?"
"How did you ever get interested in it anyway?"
"How did you happen to decide that?"

The formula will work. Try it and get used to it.

CHAPTER FIVE

The Angle— and How to Select It

In May, 1977, Monica Surfaro, a freelance magazine writer, interviewed Senator Hubert H. Humphrey in his office in the Senate Office Building in Washington. In failing health, a victim of cancer, Mr. Humphrey was then near the end of a long, distinguished career which had established him as a lively force in American politics. Rising from a clerk's job in his father's drugstore in South Dakota, he had become mayor of Minneapolis, U.S. senator from Minnesota, vice president of the United States, Democratic nominee for president, and again senator. In 1977, at age 66, he had become a venerated grand old man of American politics, a man of many, rich, and varied experiences.

Monica's task was to choose from his experiences some facet of Mr. Humphrey's life to write about in a 1500-word magazine article. She would have to focus on a relatively small spot in his lifespan and she needed some central idea around which to build the piece. During the interview, she fished for an angle, getting Mr. Humphrey to talk about one topic, then another. In addition, Mr. Humphrey volunteered information. The following is an excerpt from the transcript of the interview, the first 25 minutes of Monica's tape. From this she eventually drew the angle and most of the material for the piece.

MS: . . . One thing I was trying to figure out in your book, and I was trying to figure it out for myself but I wanted to ask you anyway, the number of people in your earlier life that were the powerful, positive forces—your grandfather, your maternal grandmother, your father, your Uncle Harry— —

HHH: Uncle Harry. He lived here in Washington—Cabin John, Maryland.

MS: Uncle Harry would be one?

HHH: Oh, a very important force in my life. Because he was the one who was constantly reminding me of the importance of my continuing my education. His letters to me are beautiful pieces of literature. I don't know if we've kept them all or not, but he wrote in a script that was absolutely marvelous. Like script writing, you know. I must have a letter of his around someplace.

From the earliest days of my acquaintance with him when I was a boy out in South Dakota, I − −

MS: Did he live in South Dakota?

HHH: Oh, no. He was from Washington, but he would come through the Dakotas because he was with the Department of Agriculture. Chief plant pathologist. And he was in charge of all of these, what we'd call experiment stations. And he would remind me of the importance of an education, and how I should proceed to a university.

MS: Do you remember any conversation − −

HHH: Oh, I stayed at his home many times when I came to Washington. The first time I ever came to Washington, I stayed at his home out at Cabin John, Maryland. If I could just get some of those letters. I suppose like many things like that that they may be tossed away, or they may be at the historical society. But . . . . I just have to ramble with you about him to give you a picture of him. You've got to keep in mind that he was a sort of folk hero, I mean, he was a childhood hero to me.

First of all, he seemed very important. He was from Washington. He could speak several languages. He had a big house which he and his own sons built. It's right out here. It's a rammed earth home. It was written up in *National Geographic*. He was the dean of the graduate school of the Department of Agriculture. He was the head man. He could write poetry. And yet when he'd come to South Dakota with us, he'd go out to the old swimming hole with us and go swimming. I mean in some filthy little old mud-bottomed swimming hole, 'cause it never rained in South Dakota.

And sometimes he'd be there on the Fourth of July, when we'd take a day off and go down to Lake Kampeska, which is the biggest lake in South Dakota. And we'd go there for a picnic.

But his emphasis to me as a young boy was clean living, lots of education, and the kind of positive thinking that you can do what you want to do. For example, he was a fellow who did not believe in smoking. And I remember when I did smoke, later on, one person I never smoked in front of was Uncle Harry. I didn't want to, the main reason was, I didn't want to offend him.

Likewise, he opened my mind − as did my father, but Uncle Harry fortified it − to what you would call the cultural life, what little we had in those days. He always believed in good music and poetry. He'd read lots of poetry to us when he'd come. He'd come out and stay two or three days, you see.

He was a religious man. Christian Scientist, as a matter of fact. Music and poetry and the arts were very much a part of his life. Just to give you a little twist of how he worked, all of his children were educated at home until the eighth grade. They educated them in their own home. And by the way, several of them are PhDs afterwards − Teddy, Hedda, Bob, Llewellyn. Four of them were PhDs in botany.

MS: You said that he taught you—maybe not taught you, but he was big in your life in the power of positive thinking.

HHH: Yes.

MS: Do you remember even any little experience that he told you about that stuck with you?

HHH: I guess I ought to be able to remember it quickly if I could.

MS: No. They were such picayune things— —

HHH: I tell you what. Yes. Here's an experience that happened. In 1931—Christmas of 1930. Christmas of 1931, yes. I was out of the University of Minnesota. I was home in South Dakota. The Depression was in full bloom there. We were ahead of everybody both in the drought, bank failures, and the Depression. Those were the only three things we ever led the nation in. I was very unhappy, restless— —

MS: You were in the pharmacy?

HHH: Yes. I was not a pharmacist yet, but I was working there in my father's store. And there was nothing really to do. And I wanted to go back to the University of Minnesota, but I didn't want to leave my father and I didn't have any money. And lo and behold, two things happened that Christmas that I almost—you know, like, providential.

Uncle Harry sent me $50. Do you know what $50 meant in those days? Fantastic! And he said, "I want you to use the $50 to go back to the university."

And the other one was my old landlady, Mrs. Zimmerman—Ma Zimmerman, we called her—Mrs. T. A. Zimmerman. She called me on the telephone—within the same week—to say, "You should come back to the university. Get out of South Dakota. And I'll give you a job in my rooming house."

'Cause she had rooms and she served breakfast. "And you can make the beds, help serve the breakfast, and I'll give you free room and board."

All that happened at a time in my life when it was really very important, because I had been at the university for a full year and had done fairly well. I was terribly discouraged that I couldn't go back, and that period of time that I was out was like all downhill.

MS: How old were you then?

HHH: I was 20 years old. Just 20.

MS: Were you with Muriel then?

HHH: No. Not yet. 1930, 31. So I was between 19 and 20. That was just a typical kind of expression, kind of act that Uncle Harry would do. He would always—in his letters to me, for example—speak of great men.

And I would write long letters to Uncle Harry. I mean, I was a romanticist in the best sense of the word, you know. I would write to him about subject matters that were far over my head, to comprehend. And he would encourage me to do that. He'd have correspondence with me.

But that $50 check resulted in me getting, within a week, out on the road, hitchhiking on the way back to the university. Now, the tuition at the university was $52, for the quarter. I had been able to get a little extra money besides, ten or 15 dollars. I went back and paid the $52 for my tuition. I had no books. I had a place to eat and sleep and I got a job—at Mrs. Zimmerman's.

MS: Did you live there?

HHH. Yes, I lived there at Mrs. Zimmerman's. I lived on the third floor, the attic.

MS: Where was that?

HHH: 528 Delaware Avenue, Southeast, Minneapolis, Minnesota. Oh, I remember that. 528 Delaware Avenue, Southeast, Minneapolis, Minnesota.

Uncle Harry was sort of in capital letters from time to time, like my father was day to day. You see, they were brothers. And you have to keep in mind that he was looked upon by myself as *the* best educated man I had ever known, a man who had really traveled a great deal, knew much. And that intrigued me. My mind was such that I liked to know people like that, 'cause I lived in a very isolated town – a town called Doland, South Dakota.

Uncle Harry in many ways was inflexible – on, like social habits. He was very flexible in terms of his relationships with me and with our family. I mean, when he came, you didn't have to dress up. You could go to the swimming hole. He was just like a real old friend.

MS: He just felt education was very important to you when he sent you the money and said you must go back?

HHH: Yes. I remember in one of his letters he had something about the definition of an educated man. I wonder if I haven't got one of those cards here. . . . Gosh. I keep a lot of things around here. I've had a whole lot of stuff. . . . Every once in a while I pull together something that. . . .

Here is that article you asked about – Woodrow Wilson, "When a Man Comes to Himself." And. . . .

Here's Uncle Harry! Come here! It's right here!

MS: I can't believe it.

HHH: By gosh.

MS: In your desk. . . .

HHH: My desk is my treasure house. Looka here. Here's his home. Right here.

MS: That was in *National Geographic?*

HHH: Yes. It was written up. This home was built by he and his sons. It's out near Cabin John, Maryland. They even built their own swimming pool. They dammed up the little creek down there. Beautiful home! Those walls are 30 inches thick. You talk about perfect insulation! In the summetime, it was as cool as if it were air-conditioned. In the wintertime, little or no heat required.

"The educated man cultivates the open mind; never laughs at new ideas; knows the secret of getting along with other people; cultivates the habit of success; knows that as a man thinketh, so is he; knows popular notions are always wrong; always listens to the man who knows; links himself with a great cause; builds an ambition picture to fit his abilities; keeps busy at his highest natural level; knows it is never too late to learn; never loses faith in the man he might have been; achieves the masteries that make him a world citizen."

Now, that's his writing.

MS: I'm noticing the handwriting. It is beautiful.

HHH: And I used to have pages of letters like this from him. You can imagine how this would impress me as a boy in school. And I longed to live at his home. My sister Frances did come. In fact, he brought her down here. He encouraged Frances to come here, and she lived at Uncle Harry's home.

And Aunt Olive, his wife, was every bit as well educated, and in many ways a more interesting person, as I got to know her later on in life.

The two of them were just precious individuals and had a very positive influence on my life – morally and from the point of view of education and what little culture, if any, I had.

MS: You said that your family never wore religion on their arm, it was just something that was part of your life?

HHH: That's right.

MS: Your mother read the Bible a lot. Did she ever read it to you?

HHH: Oh, yes. Sometimes. But we did that in church most of the time. In our little town we had Wednesday prayer night – Wednesday prayer meeting. Mother and Dad used to go to that. I'd occasionally go. But all day Sunday was Sunday school, church, and then Epworth League. And then we might go to another, different kind of church, you know, if we weren't in Doland. But there was never a Sunday that we didn't go to church. And I was in the Boy Scouts and all that sort of business as a youngster. I guess they'd call them "squares" these days.

That was a very important part of our lives. And we had as our minister the man who impressed me so much in that day, the Rev. Albert Hartt – with two t's. His son, Julian, is now a professor of philosophy at the University of Virginia. And Julian gave the prayer when I took the oath of office, as vice president. Julian and I were inseparable friends. But Doctor Albert Hartt. . . . He knew my Uncle Harry.

This little town of Doland – I tell you that it is impossible for people to believe what I'm telling you, but it had intellectual ferment that far exceeds anything that I've known anytime in my life since, except when I went to the University of Minnesota.

There were people there who were really bright. They were inquisitive; they were worldly; and they were knowledgeable. They were just great people.

Doctor Sherwood, this dear family doctor, he was a saint. He knew what real medicine was. He knew that 95 percent of medicine is healing thyself. Heal thyself. You know, these things that are written in scripture are not fiction. You've got to heal yourself, most of the time. That's what it really is, and he practiced that kind of medicine. He was there with you no matter what. There was no 40-hour week, and it wasn't that we closed up on weekends. Dear old Doctor Sherwood took care of you any hour of the day.

MS: Was he your father's doctor?

HHH: He prescribed out of our store. Doctor Sherwood and Doctor Williams. We had two doctors in that little town. You know, he operated – my God, he operated on my brother right up in his office. They didn't have all the modern tools and everything, but – –

When I look back at that little town, even today, there is that sense of pride. There are high school debating teams, high school basketball teams. There are 4-H clubs—all those things in that little town. I still get the paper, the *Times-Record*. It's still a very dynamic little community. Like so many rural towns, the external appearance doesn't look very good, but there is a quality of people there that amazes you.

I have met so many people since that I have learned how to sort out the phonies from the real ones. And those that have about one inch of culture, as compared to those who have two miles of character. You know, I'm not much on that veneer stuff. I see it all the time—all these people walking around, *uhhhh*, and they've got no character. They don't know the difference from right and wrong. I'm very impatient with them, frankly.

I haven't looked at my stuff in here for a long time.

MS: I wanted to ask you— —

HHH: This is something on how to run my indoor photography department. What in the world is this?

MS: It looks like— —

HHH: Now, here is Woodrow Wilson's acceptance speech. Nineteen hundred and. . . . For the peace prize. Now, that is really good. And then here's Saint Francis of Assisi.

What do you think Lord Keynes said when he was asked this question: "What would you do if you could live your life over again?"

He said, "Drink more champagne."

I love all those cute little remarks. All right, I know you don't want me to go through all this.

MS: Again, in going through your book looking for material. . . . I know what I would take from your life, a serious obstacle. But I would like for you to tell me, from your personal life— —

HHH: The most serious obstacle in my personal life was the Depression, which left an everlasting scar on me. I have never forgotten it because I saw what it did to people around me. I think it conditioned my whole political life and my attitude about my fellow human beings.

MS: Your father at that point was a very— —

HHH: Yes. Oh, my father was my friend, my teacher, my leader, and my loving father. I mean, he was everything to me. He was a tremendous person, a tremendous person.

MS: At that point it obviously affected the business?

HHH: Oh, yes. I saw that Depression grind him down. It literally took the lifeblood right out of him.

MS: I think in the *Ladies Home Journal* that I was reading that, that was a beautiful thing that you talked about. Could you tell me about it? I think it was that your father he wrote to you, a note or something, deciding that he couldn't take it anymore, that the business was at a point where it was so bad and I think he had gone away for a week— —

HHH: Oh, yes. He did, once, up and left. Poor Mommy. She kind of kept her suitcase packed. She never quite knew when they'd be taking a trip, you know. And I remember it was in the summer. I believe the summer of '36. Yes, I was married that summer. The summer of '37. Hot, dusty, no crops, miserable.

And I remember Dad saying to me many times, "Well, son, one thing we'll never do. They may take this business away from us, but I'm sure never going to shoot myself."

You know, it was something like that—"I'm never going to do away with myself. This is just a business." There had been so many bankers hanging themselves in that period of time——

MS: Oh, yes, I know.

HHH: One evening my Dad came into the store. I was there working. It was my night to work. He said, "Hubert, I've got to get out of here. If I stay here," he said, "I think I'll go mad. I just have to get out of here. I'm going to go home and get your mother, and we're going to take a trip."

I said, "Well, Dad, where are you going to go?"

And he said, "I don't know. But I just have to get away from here. All this is just more than I can stand right now," he said. "I want you to run the store and do the best you can."

And I said—well, I was worried about the bills, paying the bills and all.

And he said, "You just do the best you can. I'll be back. I've got to go."

It was 10 o'clock at night, between 9 and 10 o'clock at night when he got in his car, and I didn't know where he went. I knew he liked to travel out west. That's all I knew. He always liked to travel to the west. He got in his car, and the first time I heard from him, he was way out in Colorado.

And during the time he was gone, an epidemic of animal disease called anthrax broke out. My father was well known amongst rural people for vaccines and veterinary products and taking care of animals. They started—one morning—Dad had only been gone about a day or two days—and I heard a tap on the window of my little house out on Idaho Avenue, where Muriel and I lived our first few months of married life. It was 6 o'clock in the morning. There was an old farmer out there that I knew. I've forgotten his name right now, but I said, "What do you want?"

And he said, "I want to talk to you about my cattle." And he told me, he said, "They're lying—one of them's dead with black blood coming out of its nose."

And I said, "They've got anthrax." 'Cause I had been with Father many times. Anthrax spreads through a herd like mad—like the plague.

So I got up, dressed and went downtown and talked to him and asked him how many cattle he had, and he told me. And I got him enough serum and showed him how you vaccinated. Gave him——We used to loan them the serum sets, to the farmers. We'd just register them and loan them out.

And I said, "You just go out and vaccinate the rest of that herd as quick as you can, and get rid of that carcass. You have to burn the carcass."

I got on the telephone just as soon as I could get any response in Minneapolis, and I ordered up all the anthrax serum I could get—from the Anchor Serum Company, Sharp and Dohme, Parke-Davis, anybody that I knew that had anthrax serum. And I had it coming in on the train. I had a monopoly on the anthrax serum.

Well, my father heard about it about four or five days later. The news got out there. And, man, he turned around and came charging back, because all at once, of course, out of the misery of somebody else, our business had improved immeasurably.

Dad was-- I've written so much about him that it is kind of redundant to talk about him anymore. You just have to understand that he was a very, a man full of life, full of life, good humor-but also a prodigious worker. And I always felt that Dad wanted more out of life than he got.

The Necessity of an Angle

Every piece, whether a newspaper feature or magazine article, *must have an angle*. It must make some main point, or present some main message; it must be structured around some central idea.

For example, if you proposed a piece on Pope John Paul, your editor would very likely say, "What about him?" It's that "what about" that is the angle. It must be a piece on Pope John Paul as a Polish patriot, Pope John Paul and his attitudes on the church's role in the emerging nations, Pope John Paul as international peacemaker, Pope John Paul as the most traveled pope-*something specific* about Pope John Paul.

A piece must have only one angle; more than one angle is no angle. The focus of the piece ought to be sharp, not fuzzy. A piece ought not be a two-hump camel, but a one-hump camel-so the reader's mind has one clear place upon which to rest.

The angle is like a frame that contains all the pertinent material. Material not pertinent to the angle is left out of the piece.

The angle is also like a clothesline from which the piece's bits of information are hung like so many towels, T-shirts, and shorts, separate items linked by their common relationship to the line.

Or think of the angle as a Christmas tree from which dangle the parts of the piece-narrative anecdotes, lively quotes, descriptive detail-like bright, beautiful ornaments. Without the tree, they're an assortment of baubles. With the tree, they have structure, utility, and beauty, everything desirable in a feature, article, or book.

Monica Surfaro's interview with Mr. Humphrey, like his life itself, had covered a multitude of interesting people, places, and experiences. Many were attractive topics to explore with the reader. One of them or some combination of two or more naturally joined in one idea, would have to be singled out for an angle before the piece could be conceived and written. Several possibilities could be drawn from the topics raised in the interview:

1. Uncle Harry: a piece showing Uncle Harry and letting the reader see how Humphrey's life was influenced by this colorful figure.

2. Humphrey's hometown: a piece capturing Doland, South Dakota,

an authentic American scene, with dynamic influences that shaped Humphrey's attitudes.

3. The old swimming hole: a nostalgic piece showing Humphrey as a boy, against an interesting, romantic scene from a time gone by.

4. Ma Zimmerman and the boardinghouse: a piece recreating a person and place significant in the life of Hubert Humphrey, a crossroads experience that led eventually from Doland, South Dakota, to Congress and the highest councils of government.

5. Humphrey's father: a piece showing the senior Humphrey as the most important person in young Hubert's life. A possible Father's Day piece.

6. The Rev. Albert Hartt and his son Julian: a religion-in-the-life-of-Humphrey piece, letting the reader see how Humphrey was influenced by religious training as a youngster.

7. The doctor who operated on Humphrey's brother: a nostalgic piece about simpler times and ways of coping with life.

8. The drugstore: a slice-of-Americana piece, focused on Humphrey's father's store, taking the reader back to an earlier day and showing how it influenced Humphrey throughout his life.

9. The Depression: a piece about a particular place in the United States during a particularly historic time, focusing on Humphrey's own experiences with his father, the drugstore, and the community. It would let the reader see the place and the times, and how they affected Humphrey and shaped his political and social ideas.

10. The anthrax epidemic: a piece showing how Humphrey faced a critical problem on his own at an early stage in his life and its lasting effects on him.

11. Humphrey's desk and its contents: a piece letting the reader see Humphrey in his office with souvenirs and collected oddments, each of which may have something significant to say about the man.

In addition to those possible angles drawn from topics in the interview, there are angles to be drawn from combinations of the individual topics.

12. The people who influenced Humphrey: a piece linking Uncle Harry, the senior Mr. Humphrey, Ma Zimmerman, Albert Hartt, and the doctor, all colorful characters who shaped and enriched Humphrey's life.

13. Doland, South Dakota – the place and the people: a piece showing not only the town and environs (including the drugstore and the old swimming hole) but the cast of characters – the senior Humphrey, Albert Hartt, the doctor who operated on Humphrey's brother.

14. The disaster that shaped Humphrey's life: a piece combining the Depression and the anthrax epidemic, also including Humphrey's father

showing how the anthrax incident helped mold the man Humphrey was to become.

In addition to those angles, there is another one that is a possibility every time you conduct an interview:

15. The interview itself: a piece in which Humphrey and his office and the things around him would be shown to the reader from your perspective as the interviewer. Humphrey would speak to the reader just as he spoke to the interviewer. Everything significant that the interviewer saw and heard and felt would be shown to the reader, so he might come to know Mr. Humphrey, brushing shoulders with this famous person, just as the interviewer did. It is important to remember that *the interview itself is always a possible angle.*

With 15 possibilities to choose from, which do you choose? More basic, how do you decide which is best?

Analyzing the Material

Since you know you will need anecdotes, quotes, and description to make a readable piece, begin your angle selection process by analyzing the material that came from the interview. For example, what are the anecdotes? Go through the tape (or better, the transcript of the tape) and make a list, either on paper or in your head.

In the case of the Humphrey piece, make a list of the anecdotes in the transcript of Monica's interview. Then make a list of the scenes, since the piece must let the reader see the place of the action as well as the action itself. Next make a list of quotes by the various characters mentioned, including Humphrey himself when he speaks within the context of the action described in an anecdote. Such an analysis sharply reduces the number of possible angles. Whatever the angle, it must be supported by anecdotes, quotes, and description—which constitute the meat of the piece. If the interview failed to yield the material necessary to support a particular angle, that angle possibility must be discarded even though it might be a good idea for a piece.

For example, take the Uncle Harry angle. Is there an anecdote—an incident described—that shows Uncle Harry doing something? Is there a scene in which Uncle Harry appears? Is there description of Uncle Harry, so the reader can see him? Does Uncle Harry speak, except through his letters to young Hubert? There is a fragmentary anecdote about Uncle Harry and young Humphrey, when the uncle sent a letter and $50 to Hubert and urged him to go back to college. But Uncle Harry does not appear in the scene. Indeed, no scene or person is described. The only action is Hubert's opening of the envelope, implied rather than shown, and his reading the letter is not very dramatic stuff to show the reader. Uncle Harry is never described, nor does he speak, except in his letters. Clearly then, the Uncle Harry angle cannot be supported by the material and so must be discarded.

Applying the same criteria eliminates the following possible angles: (2) Humphrey's hometown; (3) the old swimming hole: (4) Ma Zimmerman and the boardinghouse; (5) Humphrey's father (the anecdote and two scenes in which he appears do not support the angle); (6) the Hartts; (7) the doctor; (8) the drugstore (the two drugstore scenes do not by themselves support the drugstore angle); (12) the people who influenced Humphrey: and (13) Doland, South Dakota, the place and the people.

The list now has been pared down to five possible angles: (9) the Depression; (10) the anthrax epidemic; (11) Humphrey's desk and its contents; (14) the disaster that shaped Humphrey's life; and (15) the interview itself. Since the disaster angle combines the Depression and anthrax epidemic angles and includes material supporting both of them, possibilities No. 9 and No. 10 may be discarded in favor of No. 14.

Of the three possibilities remaining (11) the desk and its contents, (14) the disaster, and (15) the interview itself, which is the best possibility? The same procedure that was used to eliminate Uncle Harry makes the choice clear: the disaster-that-shaped-Humphrey's-life angle. It is supported by the description of Doland, South Dakota, and of Depression times. It also includes the dramatic going-away scene and dialogue between father and son at the drugstore, the scenes with the stricken farmer at Humphrey's house and the drugstore. The scenes evoked by the farmer's quotes within the context of the action, and Mr. Humphrey's explanatory quotes outside the context of the action—including his quote about the Depression—also fit the angle.

An interview-itself angle isn't necessary when such dramatic elements arise from anecdotes told by the interview subject. In the same way, the desk-and-its-contents angle, though not without charm, becomes a pale specter next to the flesh and blood of the disaster scenes and action.

The piece to be written from the Humphrey interview, then, is something that allows the writer to take advantage of the best material—anecdotes, description, and quotes. Unless there is a good and cogent reason to do otherwise, always pick an angle that will let you use your best material. Examine what you've got, then make your choice.

Here's the way the Humphrey piece turned out. It was ghost written under Mr. Humphrey's byline, instead of the actual author's, to make it a first-person story (see section on ghost-written articles, page 115). The piece was drawn from the material obtained during Monica Surfaro's interview and from later contact with Mr. Humphrey (which included his approval of the manuscript). Another version of the story ran in the January 1978 issue of *Guideposts.*

IT WAS ABOUT 10 o'clock on a sultry August evening when my father entered the drugstore. I was running the store that night.

"Hubert," he said, and I could see the weary look in his eyes, "I've got to get away for a while. Your mother and I are leaving tonight."

It was 1937, in the dusty little town of Doland, South Dakota, and we were in the grip of the Depression, made worse in our area by a three-year drought that was forcing a lot of people to abandon their farms and ranches and move away. I was a young pharmacist then, trying to help my dad keep the family drugstore going.

A lot of the farmers and ranchers who stayed on were being carried on our drugstore accounts because Dad was too big-hearted to refuse them credit. But his own situation was so bad that he had sold his house to keep the store going.

"It's the heat and the drought," Dad said, his shoulders sagging, "and the customers who can't pay their bills and the creditors who want payment from us. I just need to get away from it for a while."

For a long time Dad had clung to a kind of dogged optimism. "The whole country is in bad shape, son," he would say. "Still, we've been through tough times before. Things have to get better." Muriel and I hadn't been married very long, and we wanted very much to believe him. But things just got worse, for nearly everyone. A lot of strong men were driven to take their own lives.

Now Dad's eyes were on me. "Hubert, I want you to run the store while we're gone," he said. "Do whatever you think needs to be done."

I'd practically grown up in the drugstore, which sold some general merchandise as well as all sorts of patent medicines, veterinary supplies and prescription drugs. But I'd always had Dad around to make the key decisions. If some kind of trouble arose, Dad was there and he seemed always to know what to do. Now all responsibility would be on me.

I immediately thought of our creditors. "But, Dad," I said, "what are we going to do about the bills? How are we going to pay them?"

They were questions Dad had no answer for. He looked at me and said wearily, "Just do the best you can, son." He then turned and strode from the store, got into his old Model A Ford and drove off into the darkness. Now I was about to find out how much I could handle.

Two days after Mom and Dad left, I was awakened around six o'clock in the morning by an urgent rapping on the bedroom window of the little house Muriel and I had rented. I got up and found that it was a farmer who had been a customer of Dad's for many years.

I opened the window and asked him, "What can I do for you?"

"Where's your father?" he said.

"He's gone on a trip," I told him. "Can I do anything for you?"

"It's my cattle," he said. "They're sick. They're all just lying around, and one of 'em's dead with black blood coming out of his nose. Can you do anything?"

I reached back into my memory, grasping for something I had seen when I had gone with Dad out into the countryside. This farmer seemed to be describing a deadly cattle disease that could go through a herd like lightning, spreading a poisonous contagion like a medieval plague. When it struck, preventive measures had to be taken at once, or it would wipe out cattle for miles around.

"Sounds like anthrax," I told the farmer. I quickly got dressed and took the farmer downtown with me and opened up the drugstore. I gave him anthrax serum to inoculate his whole herd, then got out a syringe and showed him how to use it. "And get rid of that carcass," I told him. "Burn it."

He was no sooner out of the door than I began thinking what I should do next. If I was wrong about my diagnosis of anthrax, and if it was something else that was killing the farmer's cattle, then I had only given him the wrong medicine. But if I was right, then the whole region was in trouble. If the drought and the Depression hadn't created enough economic havoc in the area, an epidemic of anthrax would wipe out everybody.

As soon as I could get the drug houses in Minneapolis to answer their phones that morning, I began calling and ordering anthrax serum—from Anchor Serum Company, from Sharp and Dohme, from Parke-Davis, from every place I could get it. And I ordered it all on credit.

When it was done, and I stood back waiting for the shipments to arrive, I found little doubts creeping into my mind. *What if it's not anthrax? What if I've bought more than we can ever pay for? What if I've misjudged?* The answer to all those tormenting questions was, I was sure, ruin for Dad's drugstore and perhaps for Dad himself as well.

Well, the serum came, and so did the customers. Muriel and I kept the drugstore open day and night, selling to farmers and ranchers and to other druggists, too. There was suddenly so much activity that the news reached Dad, who was in Colorado and read about the outbreak in a newspaper. Within four days, he came charging up to the store in the Model A, wanting to know what was going on.

By then it was obvious that we were facing a serious threat of an anthrax epidemic, and I was able to tell Dad the progress we had made to keep it in check.

In the next week or so we sold serum as fast as we could handle our customers. The cattle losses were held to a minimum, because the serum had been rushed in so quickly. And many farmers and ranchers whose businesses, like Dad's, were teetering on the edge of disaster, were spared the fatal blow that an anthrax epidemic would have dealt them. And when the farmers and ranchers came in to pay for their serum, the drugstore's money problems were tremendously eased.

Since the summer of 1937, I've gone through many crises, in politics as well as in personal life. Some of them, when I stopped to think about them too long, were enough to scare the socks off me—like the cancer surgery I underwent.

But I've been able to look back on each such situation and see good in it. It's the experiences that test us—test our abilities, our faith in ourselves, and faith in a Heavenly Father who cares—that equip us to handle life successfully.

"Just do the best you can," my Dad had told me that summer night. Over the years since then, I've tried to do that, many times. And it's amazing how often a person's best proves good enough.

Fred Welk was a fourth-year journalism student at North Texas State University when he interviewed Jim Petersen, practitioner of a rare trade. Interview completed, Fred faced the task of choosing an angle. His material was a collection of anecdotes and lively quotes, mined from the interview subject, and rich descriptive detail, gained from Fred's own observation during the interview. He decided to make the interview itself the angle, showing the subject to the reader against the background of the subject's thing (the thing that made him worth writing and reading about), weaving in his good material.

Here's part of the resulting piece, which ran in *The North Texas Daily:*

JIM PETERSEN parked his silver Ford van just inside the gate of the Estes Stables, next to the wooden building that houses the office and the tack room filled with racks of saddles and harnesses.

As if arming himself for battle, he stripped off his shirt, stepped into a pair of beige coveralls, turned his baseball cap backwards over a head of gray, thinning hair and strapped on a pair of worn, leather chaps.

"Which horse is first?" he asked, ready to begin his day's work.

Petersen is a farrier, a shoer of horses. His is the job that was left when technology blew out the blacksmith's fire.

Although his customers are spread from southern Oklahoma to south of the Dallas-Fort Worth metroplex, Petersen, 52, frequently can be found shoeing at the Estes Stables, where each year hundreds of North Texas State University students are taught horseback riding in physical education courses.

Opening the back doors of his van, he rummaged through boxes and laid his tools on a piece of burlap draped over a bucket, the way a dentist might organize his instruments on a linen covering a stainless steel tray.

The comparison is not far from truth, for a farrier is more than an equestrian manicurist and shoe salesman. He also is a bit of dentist and doctor.

"The veterinarians and the horseshoers generally have an agreement," Petersen said. "They don't shoe horses, and we don't doctor them. But you can't get away from a certain amount of shade-tree doctoring, and any working farrier who says he doesn't doctor is lying, because he does. He always has and he probably always will, simply because he deals with horses every day."

The dentistry comes in the form of "floating," or filing, a horse's teeth when they become pointed and interfere with chewing.

Petersen explained that a farrier no longer has a need to be a blacksmith. Most shoes can be bent cold and are available in various weights and sizes, making a ranch-supply house a veritable Florsheim store for horses, and a blacksmith just a picture in a history textbook.

He took the horse that was brought to him, tied it loosely to the trailer hitch of his van and poured out a box of nails. Standing alongside the animal, he lifted a foreleg and holding it securely between his own thighs, filed, clipped and cleaned the bottom of the hoof in preparation for a shoe.

"I want to make one thing very clear," he said. "A horseshoe is nothing but an extension of the outer wall of the hoof. There's no more pain than cutting your fingernails. Quite often there's more pain to the shoer than to the animal."

Petersen recalled the time he was kicked in the face.

"I was shoeing a bunch of horses in preparation for a trail ride in the spring, and there had been some real heavy rains. This was close to here, about a mile and a half away. I had a horse I wasn't acquainted with and I was shoeing him inside of a barn.

"I was just finishing up the last hoof and I heard a crack. I assumed it was thunder, but what it was was a man out back popping a whip, who I didn't realize was there.

"The horse went crazy and 'cow kicked' me in the face, raked the nails in the hoofs over me and finally kicked me away from him."

Petersen finished shoeing the horse the same hour.

It is always better to know what the angle of the story is or might be before the interview. You'll be able to focus the interview better if you know the angle, leading the subject to talk about only, or mostly, the things that pertain to it.

But there will be times when the interview will have to be a fishing expedition, and you'll hope you come up with an angle as you cast about during the conversation with the subject. If, after the interview is over, you are still unsure about the angle, carefully go through your transcript and notes, analyzing the material. See if you can find a thread that links the best anecdotes, quotes, and description.

That thread is the angle you need.

The Lead

IT WAS EARLY Tuesday morning on a soon-to-be busy road in citrus country. A police officer stepped out of the gray half-light and elbowed his way onto a battered bus filled with murmuring farm workers.

"Let me see your green card!" the thin cop shouted, blinding the workers with the glare of his flashlight. Light stabbed the face of one worker.

"You know what I'm talkin' about? Got an I-94 card? Green card?"

The worker shook his head. So did eight others. The officer termed them illegal aliens who shouldn't be in this country, who shouldn't be working in the groves. None of them had the green cards which give aliens the right to work, but nobody was arrested.

The officer's flashlight also disclosed several youngsters who appeared to be under 12. State law says children can't be in the groves—working or otherwise—without their parents.

That is the lead to a feature written by Jim Nesbitt of the Orlando, Florida, *Sentinel*. It is an *anecdotal lead*—a little story, with characters, action, and description, all the ingredients needed to make a story. The writer simply took an anecdote from his material and used it to begin the piece, thereby creating an anecdotal lead.

Van Morrison's brown, two-story, shingled house sits alongside a narrow road that snakes up Mt. Tamalpais above the sleepy Marin County town of Mill Valley. From the road, only a mailbox, with a large number that looks as if it were painted by a child, indicates the presence of Morrison's home. Down a short driveway is a tall, weathered picket fence; a chain-link fence surrounds the rest of the grounds, which are concealed for the most part by shrubbery and trees. Through the gate, one can see the house; a sloping, grass-covered hill to the right of the house ends at a long, rectangular swimming pool. A few chairs and a small stone statue of a young boy stand on the hillside among the grass.

That lead to an article Michael Goldberg did for *Rolling Stone* is a *descriptive lead*. It merely presents a scene; there are neither characters nor action, nor is it a re-creation of an incident or event. It is pure description. The writer used rich descriptive detail to begin his piece with a vivid picture for the reader.

On his honor, Buck Burshears has done his best to do his duty to God, his country and thousands of boys who've looked up to him for half a century.

The firm Layton Humphrey Jr. owns transforms brand new helicopters with appointments fit for a king or president.

Wolves took two of Gerald Brehmer's dogs. Bison forage in his crops. An inquisitive old black bear rattles around the Brehmer family trailer home, seven miles from the nearest telephone.

Kathy says there are good reasons why she spends her nights wide awake, too afraid to sleep, peering out the windows of her first-floor apartment.

For steel executives there was no place to work like Bethlehem. Salaries provided for large homes on sprawling acres, raises came regularly and there were plenty of assistants to take care of things if a manager spent an afternoon of golf at the company-subsidized Saucon Valley Country Club.

For business visitors, there was the choice of big rooms at the company-owned Bethlehem Hotel or guest quarters and golf at the company-owned Weyhill Golf Course.

And for this city, there was nothing like having Bethlehem Steel for a benevolent big brother, aiding its institutions, spearheading fund drives, helping finance civic improvements and paying for a new town hall.

The preceding leads (written, in order, by Tad Bartimus of the Associated Press, Dan Carmichael of United Press International, Bill Curry of the *Los Angeles Times,* Roberta Walburn of the *Minneapolis Tribune,* and William Robbins of *The New York Times*) may all be called *situation leads.* They are leads in which the writers attempt to present an interesting, even provocative, situation.

A couple of years ago, my friend Dudley Witney and I undertook one of the most pleasurable tasks imaginable—that of visiting a number of summer resorts all over the Untied States and Canada for the purpose of putting together a book called *Summer Places,* with photographs by Dudley and a text by me.

Every profession has its secrets and its tales. When doctors get together they gossip about miraculous recoveries and sponges left in the abdomen. Politicians discuss electoral triumphs and races lost through a slip of the tongue. Sports figures reminisce about touchdowns and fumbles, hits and errors.

New Yorkers are a race of fans and groupies. They are also compulsive critics. That they live in the arts capital of the world New Yorkers take as a matter of fact. And, as they careen from one art form to another, each decade enshrines its own kind of star, ending in the late '70s with coverpersons Midler, Barishnikov, Pavarotti, and Bocuse. *Bocuse?*

"Nontraditional student" is the catch-all term college educators use to describe just about anybody who isn't a full-time student in the 18-22 age bracket.

It has seemed almost impossible during the last several months to pick up a magazine without finding another article on the perils of being a step-parent. We even have a new word—"stepping"—to describe the condition and the process.

Those leads, which appeared on articles published in (in order) *Nautical Quarterly, The Washingtonian, The International Review of Food & Wine, Better Homes and Gardens,* and *The New York Times* may all be called *essay leads.* The writers deliver either a flat statement of fact or a bit of their own opinion.

Virtually every feature or magazine article lead may be classified in one of the four categories mentioned: anecdotal, descriptive, situation, or essay. If a lead is not one of those four, it generally is a news lead—straight information with no attempt by the writer to provoke the reader's interest in the piece, as seen in the following examples.

Union workers and representatives of 40 private, nonprofit hospitals in New York City and on Long Island averted a strike yesterday. They reached a tentative settlement that would give the workers 7½ percent raises in each year of a two-year contract, with an additional 1 percent in benefits over the life of the contract.

A proposal to increase temporarily the sales tax in Orleans Parish from 7 to 8 cents on the dollar was approved by a slim majority of voters Saturday, according to complete but unofficial returns.

Austreberia Villa, 94, widow of Mexican revolutionary hero Pancho Villa, died Monday at her home near the Caribbean coast, the official news agency Notimex reported Tuesday.

A news lead, in keeping with the fashion of inverted-pyramid news writing (arranging bits of information in a descending order of importance), is written to tell the reader all that's really necessary in the first paragraph or two. Its purpose is to spare the reader the necessity of reading the entire story.

A feature or magazine article lead should be written to achieve a completely opposite effect. It should entice the reader into reading the whole story.

It's no exaggeration to say that the lead is the most important part of the piece. The reader ordinarily will decide to read on, or not to, based on the lead. Since the whole purpose of writing is to be read, it is crucial for the writer to come up with the best lead possible in any particular piece. The writer needs to write the lead with utmost care and a keen sense of purpose, knowing that the lead is meant to be far more than merely the first paragraph of the piece.

The lead's mission is threefold: (1) attract attention, (2) introduce the subject, within the context of the angle, and (3) draw the reader into the body of the piece.

A reasonably perceptive reader, particularly if he or she is also a writer, will discern that some kinds of leads perform the lead's mission better than others. Among anecdotal, descriptive, situation, and essay leads there is an order of quality and effectiveness. One is best, one is worst, and the others are in between.

To determine that order, consider the first function of the lead – attracting attention. The lead must arouse the reader's interest. We already know that the best way to arouse interest is to present something in which the reader is already interested. Since a writer (especially a newspaper writer) is usually writing to readers with many different interests, he must turn to a universal interest to have the best chance of attracting most of the audience.

One such universal interest is, we know, *other people.* A lead with people, or a person, or some other character in it is therefore more likely to arouse interest than a lead that has none.

We also know that a story (as used in Chapter 2) is more likely to interest the general reader than is straight information – bare facts, isolated from action, description, and dialogue.

Thus the anecdotal lead is clearly best, because it's most likely to attract the reader's attention by arousing interest.

The anecdotal lead also does the best job of introducing the subject, by *showing* the subject to the reader. The anecdotal lead starts telling a story on the very first line of the piece, getting the action rolling immediately. It involves the reader with the character or characters, and the situation, in the first paragraph. The anecdotal lead is most likely to cause the reader to want to read on and thus to learn more of what happens to the characters. The reader is thus drawn into the body of the piece.

The descriptive lead is in a distant second place. The anecdotal lead shows a motion picture to the reader while the descriptive lead shows a still picture. The descriptive lead shows something and is interesting, but the reader gets just one frozen frame, no action, no characters in action. Furthermore, the descriptive lead tends to work only in pieces in which a mood or physical setting is important to the angle.

In third place is the situation lead. Its failing is that it shows the reader little or nothing, usually relying on exposition, the dullest element of writing, and a recitation of facts. Although less effective than anecdotal and descriptive leads, the situation lead often has a good reason for being used: variety. Most editors probably would not want every piece in an issue to start with an anecdotal lead – even though it does the job best – simply because they want pieces to avoid sounding alike. Like hot fudge sundaes, anecdotal leads are delicious, but how many hot fudge sundaes can a person take at one sitting?

There are other acceptable reasons for using a situation lead. You might turn to one when you have a number of anecdotes and scenes in the material that will appear in the piece, but there is no suitable anecdote or scene to serve as a lead; or when you have a suitable ancedote or scene but must write within rigid space restrictions and the anecdotal or descriptive lead takes too many words.

The worst lead is the essay lead. It is to be avoided if at all possible. The essay lead does nothing to enhance reader interest in the material or in the piece itself, serving merely as a first paragraph. It is often a sign of a sterile imagination or a barren interview, coming across to the reader in the same way an unprepared speaker does on the platform. In many cases, the essay lead indicates either inadequacy or dilettantism on the part of the writer – both leprous conditions.

Remember, before you write something other than an anecdotal or descriptive lead, that you must have a darn good reason for doing so. Make sure you're not copping out. Since situation leads are usually easier to write than anecdotal and descriptive leads, don't simply take the course of least resistance. Give the anecdotal lead a really good try before turning to something else. If your editor wants something other than the anecdotal or descriptive lead you wrote, he or she will tell you, and it will be simple enough to come up with something different then.

On the morning of January 13, 1980, a Sierra bighorn ewe (*Ovis canadensis california,* a subspecies of bighorn), her lamb and a ram stood on a rocky ledge at 10,000 feet, watching the humans below at the Pine Creek Tungsten Mine. The ewe wore a bright collar with a radio transmittter on it. Suddenly there was a loud snap followed by a muffled rumble. In less than a minute, an avalanche crashed down thousands of feet, swept the sheep off their ledge and spread out like a fan in the tailing ponds below.

The death of three of its members was another setback for the small and struggling band of nine sheep, which had been reintroduced into the species' historic range. The lamb was the third to die of the four born to the group the previous spring. In the parent herd, only 220 animals were left.

That anecdotal lead, written by Eric Hoffman for *Sierra* magazine, gives the reader a motion picture to look at as it introduces the subject. From those two paragraphs, the reader forms an idea of what the article is about: bighorn sheep or some particular aspect of bighorn sheep. And sure enough, the reader discovers it's a piece about the struggle to save bighorn sheep from the perils of man and nature.

Moving day for Tony Cuesta: the living room of his Hialeah apartment is empty, except for a folding aluminum chair, a can of Mixture No. 79 pipe tobacco and a dark suit, the one he uses for funerals and meetings with secretaries of state. The suit's hanger has been hooked on a 2-inch hole in the dry wall. Another hole is right below it.

"That's where the bullets ended up," he says blandly. Oh yes, the bullets. Some days before, two intruders had shot his bodyguard while Cuesta, blind and missing one hand, stood frozen against the wall. Holding a four-barrel .357. "It was," he says with understatement, "a very difficult moment."

Those two paragraphs form the lead of a piece that ran in *Tropic,* the Sunday magazine of the *Miami Herald.* It is an anecdotal lead, showing a scene, a character, and action (the character's dialogue constitutes action), but the reader gets no clear idea of what the piece is about. The lead is a poor one mainly because it fails to introduce the subject to the reader adequately.

In addition to attracting the reader to the piece, a lead ought to introduce the subject in the same way a proper host introduces a guest at a party. The good host presents the guest, identifies him and tells enough about him so that a conversation is set off between the guest and the person to whom he's being introduced. A good lead introduces the subject and lets the reader know enough about it to form an accurate idea of what the piece is about. The lead must introduce the subject within the context of the angle of the piece; otherwise, the lead will either misrepresent or fail to represent the piece to the reader.

The lead on the *Tropic* magazine article, for example, fails to represent the remainder of the piece, since the reader gets no clear idea of what the rest of the piece is going to be about.

Or if the *Sierra* magazine article with the lead about bighorn sheep turned out to be, on further reading, a piece about mountain avalanches, the lead would have misrepresented the piece, since the lead led the reader to believe the article was about bighorn sheep.

The writer, then, needs to select from his material an anecdote that will introduce the subject by *showing* it to the reader in a setting or action that accurately represents the rest of the piece and points the reader toward the angle of the piece. The writer might have a good, picturesque anecdote about the subject; but if it fails to introduce the subject properly, it shouldn't be used in the lead. It can be used farther down, in the body of the piece.

If the piece is about a person, the writer should look for an anecdote that shows the person doing whatever it is that makes him worth reading about (which, presumably, is also the angle of the piece). Whether choosing an anecdotal or descriptive lead, the writer must show something *specific* to the reader—a specific incident or activity in the case of an anecdotal lead or a specific scene in the case of a descriptive lead. If, for example, the writer is to show a college stadium packed with a homecoming crowd to serve as the lead to a piece on college football, the scene and action shown *must be actual,* not a composite, not hypothetical, not imagined. Writers must give the readers facts, show them reality.

If the piece is continuous narrative (one long action sequence), the writer picks an appropriate spot in the chronology of the event and starts telling the story there. The starting spot is appropriate either because it is the chronological beginning or because, though not the chronological beginning, it offers a good scene or incident to hook the reader.

For example, when John Noble Wilford wrote about the Colorado River for *The New York Times Magazine,* he chose for the lead a scene that occurred hours after the chronological beginning of the events he was to narrate in the article.

Martin Litton pulled at the oars, easing the dory into the current, and began to fulminate. We were still in sight of Lee's Ferry, where we had put in shortly after noon, after the rain clouds moved off into Utah somewhere and the hot sun dried out our little fleet.

The water was cold, no more than 50 degrees, and clear.

I dipped my Sierra cup and took a drink, more to get acquainted with the river than to quench any thirst. Litton already knew the river, with an intimacy only a boatman of many years can have, and knew enough to be concerned by the water marks he saw on rocks high along the shore. The river was low, threateningly low. "It's that dam," fumed Litton, nodding upstream in the direction of Glen Canyon Dam, 15 miles away.

Like most environmentalists, particularly those who also make a living running the rapids through the Grand Canyon, Litton has never forgiven the Bureau of Reclamation for tampering with this wildest of the big rivers in North America, the Colorado. In no uncertain terms, he blames the dam for killing mesquite trees along the shore by leaving them high and dry. He blames the dam for the fact that wind-blown tamarisk seeds are not being drowned, thus permitting these alien trees to take root in the canyon. If someone happened to burn the camp bacon, he probably would think of a reason to blame the dam for that, too. But, unquestionably, the river was low when we set out on our 18-day trip, and it was because the dam was holding back most of the spring runoff, keeping it in reserve to turn the turbines to meet "peak loads" in air-conditioned cities.

We drifted with the current at a leisurely rate of about three miles an hour—walking speed. Litton's boat kept the lead, followed by five other dories and a large inflatable supply raft.

By showing Martin Litton at the oars, the writer was able to immediately introduce the subject—the Colorado, as seen from the perspective of those who float down it in rubber rafts or wooden dories. At the same time he introduced a major character against an interesting background (the river itself) and got the action rolling in the first sentence. Then, with that character, scene, and action in the reader's mind, Wilford flashed back, in the third paragraph, to provide some background on what is happening in the lead and to bring the reader up to date on the chronology of the event. In the fourth paragraph he resumed the chronological account, which he had interrupted for the background.

The lead of the following first-person piece by Glen Taylor, published in *Charisma* magazine, managed the same technique in two paragraphs, starting not at the chronological beginning of the incident but at a more dramatic moment, then providing the reader with background information.

I was flat on my back in the shallow water, at the edge of the narrow beach, my life vest holding my face just above the chill, gentle waves, which I could feel sloshing in my ears and against my cheeks. Below my upper arms and shoulders, I couldn't feel anything, couldn't move anything. My head seemed to be lying apart from my body, detached, and my neck was solid pain.

By now Rusty, my brother-in-law, at the wheel of the boat that had sped me across the lake on water skis, had swung the boat in to shore and leaped out to see why I hadn't gotten up after my spill, after my ski had snagged in the sand in the shallow water and I had cartwheeled into the air and landed hard on the back of my neck.

Then, following the background material, the author returned to the chronological account:

My wife Susan, eight months pregnant, climbed from the boat and followed Rusty, the two of them splashing toward me as some of the people on the beach waded toward me, too.

In other cases, it will seem more appropriate to begin the piece at the chronological beginning of the event, as in this lead to an article about a tornado that struck the high school in DeSoto, Texas, told from the perspective of the school's principal.

At 6:30 that morning, Bob Browning was thinking of what he had coming up that day. He had no appointments, he knew, with anybody from the outside, that world of parents and PTA and school board and civic groups and city officials and media people, that could rise up to challenge and criticize. He thus had no need to wear the uniform—suit and tie and shiny shoes—and be uncomfortable.

It was too late in the semester for that sort of thing anyway—only three weeks till summer vacation. This was the time to slow up, wind it down, let the year come to a nice and easy end.

Browning was ready for it, like the teachers and the kids. So instead of the suit and tie, he chose slacks and a sweater.

In the kitchen, he swallowed the coffee, kissed his wife Chris, a teacher herself, and the girls goodbye, nine-year-old Macy and six-year-old Amy, who'd be leaving for school pretty soon, too, then stepped out of the house.

The morning was cool and gray, he vaguely noticed, about 65 degrees, mildly windy, as it often is on the treeless plains of north Texas.

That continuous-narrative article recounted the entire event chronologically, with no flashbacks, using exposition, woven into the narrative, to provide background to the reader.

An effective lead might be no more than a sentence, such as this situation lead by Erin O'Brien:

> The name on her black, sequinned T-shirt said, "Phaedra," and the long jeweled earrings and the painted spot between her eyes said she was different all right.

Another effective lead might go on for 500 words or more, such as this anecdotal lead from a piece by Peter Kerasotis that ran in *Today,* the daily newspaper serving the Cocoa, Florida, area.

It was mid-morning at Al Lopez Field in Tampa and the rising sun had not yet burned away the low-lying gray clouds that shrouded the spring-training complex in dampness.

The Cincinnati Reds baseball team, directed by a blond young man in red shorts and a white shirt, ambled through a series of stretching exercises.

The mood was relaxed. Two Spanish-speaking players maintained a running dialogue. Younger players—the hopefuls—stuck together in a quiet pack. The pitchers, sitting reverently behind Tom Seaver, gathered in a large herd closest to left field. Johnny Bench sat in front of Seaver, half-heartedly going through the exercises. But like the head lion, he kept a watchful eye over the rest of the players.

Clint Hurdle, the former Merritt Island High School football and baseball star who was traded from the Kansas City Royals during the off season, was stretching out by himself in the very back of the pack. He sat on the ground with legs spread, alternately touching his fingertips to the toes of his cleated shoes. He was bent over, holding the toe of his left shoe, when the homosexual jokes started rolling from his teammates.

Shortstop Dave Concepcion inadvertently started the bench-jockeying when he said something about not having had sex since reporting to camp. "You've only been here less than a week," one player said. Concepcion replied that he woke that very morning feeling especially frisky.

"Have you talked to Clint yet?" catcher Mike O'Berry blurted out from his spot near the pitchers.

The players, all 40 of them, erupted in laughter. Hurdle turned around, his deeply tanned face reddening. He also was laughing.

The next exercise had the players on their hands and knees, their bottoms exposed. "Watch out for Hurdle," one of the players called out. This time the laughter was deeper, heartier. O'Berry rolled to his side and onto his back, laughing. Hurdle bowed his head as if to hide embarrassment.

The blond young man in red shorts instructed the players to kick their legs out and up while they were on their hands and knees. "This is just like ballet," Seaver said. Then the players were told to find a partner for the next exercise. "Oh goody," Seaver said. "Now we get a partner."

Before the chuckles subsided, Bench jumped up from the ground and skipped and pranced his way to Hurdle. He threw his arm around the taller ballplayer and raised his left arm in a cute ballet pose before letting his wrist fall limp. The players were hysterical now as two photographers posted themselves in front of Bench and Hurdle, snapping pictures as fast as their thumbs could flick the film-advance lever.

The exercise session disbanded shortly thereafter, the players scurrying to one of four practice fields. Moments later, Bench, with helmet on head and bat in hand, stood outside a batting cage waiting his turn. He was asked about the ribbing he and his teammates levied on Hurdle. He also was asked about the rumors—malicious as they were—which swirled around Hurdle during the end of the 1981 season and on past the World Series.

The rumors associated Hurdle's name with homosexuality.

"It's a bunch of bull— — —," Bench said suddenly and forcefully.

If there is any hard rule about the length of a lead, it is that a short piece should have a short lead and a long piece may have a long lead. Erin O'Brien's piece on the Florida belly dancer who called herself Phaedra was approximately 1000 words. Peter Kerasotis's piece on Clint Hurdle ran about 3000 words. A good rule of thumb on lead length is that a lead should constitute no more than 10 percent of the piece (though Kerasotis exceeded that, with no injury to the piece).

The lead is a literary device that the writer uses with deliberateness to attract the attention of the reader, introduce the subject to the reader within the context of the angle, and draw the reader into the piece.

Ordinarily, the best ways to achieve the lead's objectives are:

1. Write an anecdotal lead that *shows* the subject in relation to his, her, or its thing. Give the reader a character, or characters, to identify with, put the character in action, and let the reader see it all by providing description.

2. Make every effort to come up with an anecdotal lead, but if there is no anecdote suitable for the lead, write a descriptive lead or a situation lead, whichever seems more appropriate.

3. Make sure the lead recreates a specific, actual incident or scene.

4. In the case of a continuous-narrative piece, use as a lead a dramatic or chronologically appropriate incident or scene.

5. Limit the lead to about 10 percent of the length of the piece.

6. Always remember the importance of the lead and what you're trying to accomplish with it—and write accordingly.

The Justifier

EVERY PIECE needs a reason for being.

It needs a reason for a writer to write it, a reason for an editor to accept it and run it, a reason for a reader to read it.

The first reader who must see the reason is, of course, the editor who has the power to accept or reject the piece. There must be something about the subject of the piece that will make it worth reading about, that will satisfactorily answer the question, "So what?"

For many pieces, especially newspaper features, that something is called *newsworthiness*. Most newspaper editors and many magazine editors will insist a piece be newsworthy before they will accept it or schedule it for publication. The more newsworthy the subject, the more likely the piece is to be accepted and published.

The reader who sees the piece in the publication also should be given a reason to read it. He or she must somehow come to believe the piece is going to be worth the time and effort required to read it, and that belief should come early in the piece.

The part of the piece that suggests the reason to read it may be called a *justifier*. It justifies, or attempts to, the writer's writing the piece, the editor's publishing it, and the reader's reading it. The justifier comes near the beginning of the piece, as close to the lead as possible, so the reader sees it as soon as possible.

For example, read again the lead to John Noble Wilford's article on the Colorado River:

Martin Litton pulled at the oars, easing the dory into the current, and began to fulminate. We were still in sight of Lee's Ferry, where we had put in shortly after noon, after the rain clouds moved off into Utah somewhere and the hot sun dried out our little fleet.

The water was cold, no more than 50 degrees, and clear. I dipped my Sierra cup and took a drink, more to get acquainted with the river than to quench any thirst. Litton already knew the river, with an intimacy only a boatman of many years can have and knew enough to be concerned by the water marks he saw on the rocks high along the shore. The river was low, threateningly low. "It's that dam," fumed Litton, nodding upstream in the direction of Glen Canyon Dam, 15 miles away.

Like most environmentalists, particularly those who also make a living running the rapids through the Grand Canyon, Litton has never forgiven the Bureau of Reclamation for tampering with this wildest of the big rivers in North America, the Colorado. In no uncertain terms, he blames the dam for killing mesquite trees along the shore by leaving them high and dry. He blames the dam for the fact that windblown tamarisk seeds are not being drowned, thus permitting these alien trees to take root in the canyon. If someone happened to burn the camp bacon, he probably would think of a reason to blame the dam for that, too. But unquestionably, the river was low when we set out on our 18-day trip, and it was because the dam was holding back most of the spring runoff, keeping it in reserve to turn the turbines to meet "peak loads" in the air-conditioned cities.

We drifted with the current at a leisurely rate of about three miles an hour – walking speed. Litton's boat kept the lead, followed by five other dories and a large inflatable supply raft.

Now, here come the justifier – the suggestion of a reason to keep on reading. It is the author's answer to the inevitable question that the reader forms in his mind and that the editor demands of the writer: "So what?"

We were a party of 33 – seven boatmen, a cook, and 25 passengers. We were doing what several thousand people do each summer, casting away from ordinary comfort and security, and seeking an elemental experience in the risks of white water and the grandeur of canyon depths.

In the justifier, the author attempted to attach significance to his subject, importance to the events the piece is to describe. The justifier suggests that the story is not about a singular, isolated incident without relevance or meaning to other humans. The experience that the piece will describe is something that thousands do every summer; in other words, a lot of people are affected by this thing. Besides that, the justifier suggests this experience has adventure and romance, even a touch of mystery – thus holding out to the reader three of the five "fundamentals" in which William Randolph Hearst said people are interested.

Here are some other examples of justifiers:

The lead.

by Fred Welk

Jim Petersen parked his silver Ford van just inside the gate of the Estes Stables, next to the wooden building that houses the office and the tack room filled with racks of saddles and harnesses.

As if arming himself for battle, he stripped off his shirt, stepped into a pair of beige coveralls, turned this baseball cap backwards over a head of gray, thinning hair and strapped on a pair of worn, leather chaps.

"Which horse is first?" he asked, ready to begin his day's work.

The justifier.

Petersen is a farrier, a shoer of horses. His is the job that was left when technology blew out the black-smith's fire.

Although his customers are spread from southern Oklahoma to south of the Dallas-Fort Worth metroplex, Petersen, 52, frequently can be found shoeing at the Estes Stables, where each year hundreds of North Texas students are taught horseback riding in physical education courses.

Fred Welk's piece on the farrier was written for and published in the *North Texas Daily,* the campus newspaper of North Texas State University. Therefore it was important for him to establish relevance with North Texas students, which he did in the justifier. The justifier also performed the task of telling the reader what was going on in the lead and hinting at what was to come.

The lead.

by Jim Nesbitt
Orlando Sentinel

LAKE ALFRED — It was early Tuesday morning on a soon-to-be busy road in citrus country. A police officer stepped out of the gray half-light and elbowed his way onto a battered bus filled with murmuring farm workers.

"Let me see a green card!" the thin cop shouted, blinding the workers with the glare of his flashlight. Light stabbed the face of one worker.

"You know what I'm talkin' about? Got an I-94 card? Green card?"

The worker shook his head. So did eight others. The officer termed them illegal aliens who shouldn't be in this country, who shouldn't be working in the groves. None of them had the green cards which give aliens the right to work, but nobody was arrested.

The officer's flashlight also disclosed several youngsters who appeared to be under 12. State law says children can't be in the groves — working or otherwise — without their parents.

The justifier.

The scene underscored the mammoth problems facing farm labor law enforcement. The Florida State Employment Service, which enforces state labor laws, has only two officers covering Polk and Osceola counties, the state's largest citrus region with an estimated 2,000 crew chiefs and 20,000 farm laborers.

And the officer's actions during this pre-dawn roadblock, where the foggy dark was pierced by the eerie flash of the magnesium flares, typified how the job is handled — hit the violations you can do something about and let the others slide.

The lead.

by Ronald B. Taylor
Los Angeles Times

Night darkened the cab as Kathy Manning downshifted the big 18-wheeler and pulled off the freeway, queuing up behind other trucks at the Castaic, Calif., scales along Interstate 5.

She let the 72,500-pound semi-tractor and trailer roll slowly across the scales, got the green clearance light for the load of metal ceiling grids and gunned the powerful diesel.

Checking her mirrors for oncoming traffic, she wheeled the rig onto the freeway. As she shifted up through the gears, Manning yelled over the engine's roar: "If I ever meet a man I can love, I'll settle down, quit drivin' truck."

She took a pinch of snuff, tucked it between her lower lip and gums and continued, "But this is something I can do. I've mastered it. I'm a truck driver and I like it."

Here, at the beginning of a long, looping trip that would carry her through four states in eight days, is where Manning is happiest. The anticipation of new places and the chance meetings with old friends filled her talk.

From British Columbia to the Great Salt Lake, over-the-road drivers call her "Sweet Drifter" and describe her as that "pretty little thing" who stands just over 5 feet tall and doesn't weigh more than 105 pounds.

The justifier.

Manning, soon to be 30, is one of a small but growing number of women who drive trucks for a living.

However, most of these women drive local hauls or work as part of two-driver teams, typically a husband and wife, driving as owner-operators of long-haul trucks.

"It's very, very rare to see a woman driving alone over the road. It's hard, lonely work," said an officer of the California Highway Patrol at the Castaic scale.

Manning is one of the solo, long-haul drivers. . .

The following is a justifier that follows a descriptive lead, from an article that ran in *Rolling Stone.*

The lead.

by Timothy White

The window shades are drawn against the late-summer sun, transforming the suite in Manhattan's genteel old Carlyle Hotel into a lonesome oasis of resignation not unlike the sitting room of a sanitarium. Is is perfectly quiet within—no, there is the faint wheeze of labored breathing. Hunched in a stuffed easy chair at one end of the long living room is a pillowy mound of a man dressed in crisply pressed cotton pajamas and a linen bathrobe, his small feet reposing in scuffed leather slippers, his thin hair neatly combed. He appears to be asleep, his round, pink head pitched forward, chin upon the barrel chest, plump arms laying against his thick waist. If not for his size and the silvery stubble that coats his jaws, he might be one of Maurice Sendak's man-faced infants, dreaming inside the frames of the illustrator's pleasantly baroque picture fables.

The justifier.

How does one awaken James Cagney, one of the finest and most versatile talents in the annals of cinema? Surely, at the age of eighty-two, with half a century of stardom (and twenty years of retirement) behind him, he desires and deserves his rest. But the consequences of living so long and rising so high in his profession have conspired against him.

Here are justifiers that follow situation leads.

The lead.

by Bill Curry
Los Angeles Times

DELTA JUNCTION, Alaska— Wolves took two of Gerald Brehmer's dogs. Bison forage in his crops. An inquisitive old black bear rattles around the Brehmer family trailer home, seven miles from the nearest telephone.

And now, after an initially promising growing season, Brehmer's amber waves of grain are white with a crusty bed of snow, the broken staffs of barley lost to the elements.

The justifier.

With 19 other families, Brehmer, 31, and his wife Cynthia, 30, are trying to bring large-scale agriculture to a new land and to open a new frontier. "We're pioneering," declared 65-year-old John Emery, who is also among this tiny band of farmers. "It's all new here," he added, after a season in which most of his crop was lost to the weather. "That's the drawback to pioneering."

One hundred miles southeast of Fairbanks, on 59,700 acres of good soil once covered by black spruce and moss, these latter-day pioneers are participating in a bold new venture that brings together two of the predominant issues in Alaska: money and land.

The lead.

by Tad Bartimus
Associated Press

LA JUNTA, Colo.—On his honor, Buck Burshears has done his best to do his duty to God, his country and thousands of boys who've looked up to him for half a century.

The justifier.

James Francis (Buck) Burshears is the only leader Boy Scout Explorer Troop 2230 has ever had. He founded it in February 1933 with 27 members and one motto: "You don't have to wait to be a man to be great. Be a great boy."

Burshears is a big man with a hearty voice, a fat cigar and a ready handshake. Now, at 72, the childless widower looks back on the years he dedicated to teaching other men's boys how to become men.

His devotion to "his kids" has brought him an honorary doctorate from the University of Colorado, along with scouting's highest honor, the "Silver Buffalo."

The justifier is an indispensable part of every feature and article. You should write the justifier so that it performs all three of its functions:

1. Tell the reader what's going on in the lead. Although a good lead suggests what the piece is about, the writer ordinarily must include something that will confirm what the lead suggests. Whether it's an anecdotal, descriptive, or situation lead, some explanation is usually needed so the reader knows for sure what the action, scene, or situation in the lead is all about. The explanation is exposition. It is the writer *telling* the reader. And it comes just under the lead.

2. Establish newsworthiness or relevance. The justifier points out the importance of the subject, giving the reader a good reason to keep reading.

3. Hint at what is to come. An effective justifier offers a promise of what the reader will discover by reading on, thereby drawing him deeper into the piece.

Organization: Outlining and Putting the Piece Together

STEWART ALSOP, a frequent contributor to the old *Saturday Evening Post,* a book author, and onetime Washington columnist with his brother Joseph, once wrote for the old *Post* an article on writing articles. Unfortunately for his posterity of writers, the piece was never published, and most of Alsop's valuable insights were lost. One of them, however, stuck in my mind as the manuscript passed through my hands in the *Post's* editorial offices, where I was then a junior-type editor.

Alsop had struggled with the enormity of forming a readable, coherent, 5,000-word article from an amorphous mass of factual information and discovered that, like any other complex task, building an article could be simplified by dividing the article into parts. Those parts he called chunks.

He suggested writing chunk by chunk. The writer was not to worry about writing the entire piece; instead he should concentrate on just one part, seeing it clearly, sorting out the material needed, and writing that one chunk before moving on to the next (knowing what was to come but making the next chunk wait its turn).

It's the best kind of advice. Gathered facts, accumulated from interviews, previously published material, and the writer's own observations, can form a literal mound of tapes, transcripts, clips, Xeroxed pages, folders, publicity handouts, handwritten notes, tear sheets. From that mound must come a readable, coherent piece, not merely facts spread crudely onto blank paper or into a VDT. The writer must plan how to present the chunks of material in a logical, make-sense, what-do-I-need-to-tell-the-reader-next sequence. That sequence should be thought out in advance of the writing itself. When the writer sits down to his typewriter or VDT, he should do so with an outline of the piece, ready to follow the outline like a road map, knowing where he wants to go, how to get there and how long it will take. He should start the trip only after deciding exactly the route to follow. Doing so will save time and effort and yield a better result all around.

If you made an outline prior to the interview (always a good idea), the task now, before writing starts, is merely to adjust the outline to accommodate the gathered material. If there was no outline then, now's the time to make one. Skilled writers often devise outlines in their heads, and can visualize the finished piece, as an architect can his completed edifice, before construction starts. For beginning and developing writers, however, the best policy is to put the outline on paper, since it forces them to see the piece's components—the chunks—and to arrange them in an orderly, logical sequence. Outlining is the best way to proceed, whether the piece is a relatively uncomplicated, one-source feature or a complex, wide-ranging, multi-source magazine article or book. The job is always made easier by reducing the piece to a series of chunks.

Making an outline is a chore many writers would like to avoid. It requires mental effort, and no labor is more dreaded than mental labor (why else do writers dust their desks, clean their typewriters, empty wastebaskets, sharpen pencils, perform almost any manual task to forestall the moment when they must face blank copy paper or an empty VDT screen?). Yet in every case before writing, a writer must grapple with (1) the angle, forcing himself, to answer the question, "What is this piece about?" and (2) the organization, forcing himself to answer a second question: "What's the best way to tell this story?"

In many cases, the material and angle will help answer the latter question. For example, the story of how a Maryland National Guard officer found and rescued an eight-year-old boy lost in a state park is best told chronologically, reconstructing the event for the reader in the same sequence in which it unfolded in reality. However, the story of how a paper manufacturing company's proposal to mine peat from a swamp might affect an adjoining lake, its wildlife, and nearby residents is a more complicated matter.

The Basic Outline

The first two parts of every outline are the same: (1) the lead and (2) the justifier. All pieces follow a certain bare-bones outline: (1) Lead; (2) Justifier; (3) Body of the piece; and (4) Conclusion. The body-of-the-piece section, the heart and substance of the piece, requires special thought and planning. It is always the biggest part of the piece, made up of at least several chunks.

CONTINUOUS NARRATIVE AND ACTION INTERVIEW PIECES. The task of organization is relatively simple with some pieces. For example, a continuous narrative article or feature usually presents the material in chronological order, unfolding the story to the reader in the same sequence, more or less, that it unfolded in reality. The piece opens with an anecdotal lead (see Chap. 6, the continuous narrative lead), then presents the justifier, returns to the action where it was interrupted for the justifier, and proceeds chronologically to the end of the story.

The same more or less chronological sequence of presentation is applicable for the piece whose angle is the interview itself, especially an action interview. Recall Fred Welk's piece on the farrier in Chap. 5. Welk gathered his material in an action interview, observing the subject at work while eliciting information from him through conversation and questioning. As the angle, Welk used the interview itself, building the entire piece around a re-creation of the interview. He introduced the subject in the lead, offered the reader a justifier, then proceeded into the body of the piece, reeling out the material in roughly the same sequence he had reeled it in during the interview.

The lead.

Jim Petersen parked his silver Ford van just inside the gate of the Estes Stables, next to the wooden building that houses the office and the tack room filled with racks of saddles and harnesses.

As if arming himself for battle, he stripped off his shirt, stepped into a pair of beige coveralls, turned his baseball cap backwards over a head of gray, thinning hair and strapped on a pair of worn, leather chaps.

"Which horse is first?" he asked, ready to begin his day's work.

The justifier.

Petersen is a farrier, a shoer of horses. His is the job that was left when technology blew out the blacksmith's fire.

Although his customers are spread from southern Oklahoma to south of the Dallas-Fort Worth metroplex, Petersen, 52, frequently can be found shoeing at the Estes Stables, where each year hundreds of North Texas students are taught horseback riding in physical education courses.

The body of the piece.

Opening the back doors of his van, he rummaged through boxes and laid his tools on a piece of burlap draped over a bucket, the way a dentist might organize his instruments on a linen covering a stainless tray.

The comparison is not far from truth, for a farrier is more than an equestrian manicurist and shoe salesman. He is also a bit of a dentist and doctor.

"The veterinarians and the horseshoers generally have an agreement," Petersen said. "They don't shoe horses, and we don't doctor them. But you can't get away from a certain amount of shade-tree doctoring, and any working farrier who says he doesn't doctor is lying, because he does. He always has and he probably always will, simply because he deals with horses every day."

The dentistry comes in the form of "floating," or filing, a horse's teeth when they become pointed and interfere with chewing.

Petersen explained that a farrier no

longer has a need to be a blacksmith. Most shoes can be bent cold and are available in various weights and sizes, making a ranch-supply house a veritable Florsheim store for horses, and a blacksmith just a picture in a history textbook.

He took the horse that was brought to him, tied it loosely to the trailer hitch of his van and poured out a box of nails. Standing alongside the animal, he lifted a foreleg and, holding it securely between his own thighs, filed, clipped and cleaned the bottom of the hoof in preparation for a shoe.

By using the interview as an angle, the writer obtains a natural structure for the piece. He presents the material in the same sequence it was presented during the interview. However, the writer is apt to find that strictly following such an order of presentation may cause repetition, because the interview left, then returned to some topic. Following that order may not give the information in the sequence needed if the reader is to understand it. Sometimes the information may not come in a logical sequence.

In the farrier piece, Welk presented the action part of the interview chronologically, and the elicited material was woven into the account of the interview following a logical rather than a chronological sequence of presentation.

The piece followed this outline:

1. Explanation of what a farrier is.
2. Explanation of what a farrier does.
3. Experiences of being a farrier.

It was important for the writer to give the reader some fundamental information about farriers and horseshoeing before moving into the anecdotal material. The reader would have to have that information to accurately picture the farrier at work and readily understand the narrative and anecdotes that illustrated the life and work of a farrier. Welk used a logical, what-should-I-tell-the-reader-next sequence of presentation of the elicited material.

In a similar way, author Terrie Riecke wrote about the life of a garbage man in Gainesville, Florida. She planned the piece to be a sort of day-in-the-working-life-of-a-garbage-man article. She conducted an action interview, observing the garbage man, Fred Strong, doing his thing (and like Welk, became a source herself), and eliciting additional material from him for explanation, background, insight, and knowledge that could not come by mere observation during the action interview. Riecke began the piece where the interview itself began, like this:

The lead.

It was 6:30 a.m., and the sun was just beginning to peep above the horizon as the grumblings and groanings of 35 trucks shaking off their sleepiness rose with the morning mist. Men clad in blue work pants and thick brown boots waved and called to one another, shouting bets about who would finish the work day first. Some leaned into battered cars to kiss wives goodbye before they turned, boots crunching their way through the white-sand-and-shell parking lot, and made their way to the grumbling monster trucks whose bellies were ready to be filled with up to 20,000 pounds of refuse.

The justifier.

While most people in Gainesville were still hugging their pillows or just beginning a leisurely morning shower, these men were setting out on a hard, dirty, sweaty, smelly day that could last until 10:30 p.m., laboring to dispose of the waste other people had created, of the junk that no longer had a use. They are Gainesville's garbage men.

The body of the piece.

Fred Strong is such a man. Despite the heat of the morning, he had a blue knit cap pulled low over his head, allowing only a few corn-rowed strands of hair to peep out from underneath. His dark blue pants fell low over his heavy, brown work boots, and he sported a faded blue T-shirt with a faded red collar. Bold black letters declared, "Garbage Power," from the shirt's front.

"Garbage power, huh?" I teased as I met him. He extended his hand for a firm handshake.

"You better believe it, baby," he said, grinning broadly to show a flash of bright-white teeth. "Let's get going."

Strong, 30, is one of 55 garbage men employed by Browning-Ferris Industries, the largest waste system company in the world. Since October, 1977, BFI has had the exclusive contract to haul Gainesville's trash, and Strong has been helping them do it for the past two years.

Strong's partner, Scott Nissen, a tall, thin, blond-haired neophyte to the garbage business, has been working for BFI for two months.

"But he can run for that garbage with the best of them, that Tweety," Strong said proudly. "I call him Tweety because he reminds me of that bird in the cartoons, you know," Strong explained. "We all give each other nicknames out here. Soon he'll be thinkin' of one for me."

We crunched our way to the truck that would be our home for the next eleven hours, a 23,000-pound, 18-cubic-yard, $70,000 construction of steel whose hydraulic compression can squeeze 800 pounds of garbage into each cubic yard of its hollow belly. Larger trucks at BFI can pack more than 1,000 pounds of trash per cubic yard.

Nissen extended his hand to help me into the black vinyl interior of the truck. There was plenty of room for the three of us, despite the five-speed gear shift and the large red-and-yellow cooler filled with Gatorade that BFI gives its employees each day. A citizen's band radio hung from the cracked dashboard.

"No regular radio," Strong said, shifting the truck into first gear. "Management says it distracts us from the job, but it wouldn't me. I love music." He flashed a smile and turned the big wheel of the truck to head out for the day.

The truck began to roll along its bouncy journey across the open-field parking lot behind the long, white trailer that is BFI headquarters, jostling our bodies with its swaying, lumbering motion.

"Just like ridin' a horse, isn't it?" Strong said, and laughed the first of many, wide-grinned, teeth-flashing, throaty laughs he would offer during the day.

As his right hand swung the faded black steering wheel to the left from N.W. 55th Place onto Highway 441, Strong raised one eyebrow and asked skeptically, "You really doing a story on a garbage man? Man, I can't believe that. That's really somethin'. You gonna use our names?"

To my nod he leaned across the wheel to tap Nissen on the shoulder.

"How 'bout that. We're gonna be famous. I'll buy all the copies." Again, the throaty laugh.

To that, Nissen offered a quiet suggestion: "Just tell them they overstuff their cans."

Nissen explained that BFI has a rule limiting the weight of garbage cans to 40 pounds. Anything heavier is supposed to be left behind, he said. Any man hurting his back by lifting a too-heavy can pays the consequences by losing work days. That means losing money.

"But people always stuff their cans too much and complain if we don't pick them up," Nissen said, sighing.

The air brakes of the truck squeaked us into our first stop, a single-story white house with ten brown-paper bags on its well-kept lawn. Strong and Nissen pulled on thick canvas gloves that still managed to hint that they once were white, and hopped out of the truck. Trotting to the rear of the truck, they each grabbed two bags at a time, tossing them into the belly of the truck. Nissen, who is the "hopper"—the man who rides hanging onto the back of the truck, often jumping off to scoop up trash cans and empty them into the truck before it has stopped—stayed behind to climb onto his rear-bumper perch as Strong ran back to the cab of the truck.

To a garbage man, time is everything, Strong said in explanation of why they run to get the trash.

"We just want to get the job done well in a hurry, because when we're through, the day is ours, no matter what time it is. If we finish the route at two o'clock, then we're through workin' at two o'clock, and that's all right with me," he said.

"But the same goes if we don't finish until ten at night. You work until you're through. So it's best to work out some kind of system with your partner so you can get the trash without wasting any time. Like if I see there's just one

bag by the side of the road, I won't even stop the truck 'cause Tweety can just lean over the side and swoop that baby up without gettin' off the truck. That's the kind of trash I like," he said, grinning broadly.

Strong also explained that he gets paid for 40 hours a week, whether or not he works that long. Any overtime is paid at a time-and-a-half rate.

"So we don't stop to eat lunch or dinner or anything like that," Strong said. "We just work until we're through, then go home and make up for it with a nice big dinner. Me, I don't like to eat breakfast or anything in the morning. That just makes me feel lazy. I save up my eating for when the day's through."

Though they have been working together for only two months, Strong and Nissen have a well-established system of signals to make their work day go more swiftly. A certain type of whistle from Strong lets Nissen know that a back-door pickup—trash to be picked up in the back yard of a house rather than at the curb—is coming up and to be ready to jump off the truck and run for it. Strong will jump out of the truck to pick up trash at the curbs of nearby houses until Nissen returns with the back-door pickup.

"It's mostly senior citizens or handicapped people who get back-door," Strong said, showing me a list of 41 names on his route that get the service. "But some folks with money pay extra for it so they won't have to carry their garbage down. I don't understand why, but they'd rather pay than just carry it to the curb," he said, shaking his head.

Other whistles Strong uses alert Nissen that cars are coming or that trash is in a hidden place, like behind a car in a driveway.

"You'd be surprised at what people do with their trash sometimes," he said, laughing. "They put it behind cars, behind bushes, behind trees, where we can't always see it. Then they'll call up the office and complain if we happen to miss them."

Strong guided the truck past a house with garbage littering the lawn.

Riecke recreated the interview, taking the reader inside the garbage truck with her to see and hear Fred Strong and Scott Nissen, reeling out the quotes and sights and incidents in more or less the same order in which she had observed them. She decided which bits of information about the garbage men the reader needed to know first and wove them into the re-creation of the action, giving a gradually more complete picture of her subject as the piece carried the reader through the day.

PROFILES. Most features and articles about a person—profiles or personality sketches—including Terrie Riecke's piece about the garbage man, can follow one basic outline, like this:

1. Lead
2. Justifier
3. Present ⎫
4. Past   ⎬ Body of the piece
5. Other ⎪
6. Future ⎭
7. Conclusion

Following the justifier, the piece would show the subject doing his or her thing—the thing that makes him or her newsworthy and worth reading about. In the case of the garbage man, the thing is Fred Strong's doing his job as the driver on a garbage truck. In the case of the farrier, it is Jim Petersen's doing his job as a farrier. Of course it is not always the subject's occupation that is his thing. It is whatever the angle of the piece dictates. An article about how Ronald Reagan uses his ranch as a vacation retreat, for example, would show him at leisure around the ranch. A piece on Paul Newman as a race car driver would show Newman in connection with racing, not acting.

It only makes sense that since the piece is about Paul Newman, race car driver, the piece show him as a driver. It makes sense, too, that racing anecdotes, scenes, quotes, and other current race driving information about Newman constitute most of the body of the piece. It makes further sense to present that material as soon as possible—right after the lead and justifier.

Material that shows—and when necessary, explains—the subject doing his thing will ordinarily show him doing it now, in the present. The present in most cases will actually stretch back a bit in time, perhaps months, even years. It may also extend into the future—next month or even next year—handling material about an event that has not yet occurred. The present fills a time frame large enough to include enough· material to adequately cover the subject's newsworthy thing.

Once the reader has seen and heard that, it's natural for him to want to know when and how and where it all began, so the writer at that appropriate spot in the piece presents the past, or background, material.

If the angle, however, is *how* Paul Newman became a successful race driver, the past section will be longer, by far, than the present section. Generally the present section will be longer, however.

By the time a reader has read through the first four sections of the piece, he has become more than a little interested in the subject. Good pieces—which are always made from good material—generate as well as satisfy interest in the subject. After the section on the past, the reader should be deeply involved in the life of the person in the piece and want to know something about the person *as a person* (as distinguished from the person as the doer of his or her newsworthy thing).

At that point the writer presents personal material—information about the subject's family, life-style, other interests, whatever will help the reader feel better acquainted with the subject. There may be material besides the personal stuff that is worth including, too, especially if there is an anecdote or quotes too good to be left out of the piece. Such material can go into the "other" section.

At this point in the article, the reader has been told nearly all that is pertinent and interesting, within the limits of the piece's length. Now the reader is ready to learn where the subject goes from here—what's likely to happen next, what the plans call for, and so forth. So the writer now presents the material about the subject's future, in most cases a brief but important section of the piece.

After that, there's just one remaining section to be presented: the conclusion. Chapter 9 will take up that section of the piece.

Stock Solutions to Organization

Many pieces-to-be, because of their subject matter, defy a quick or simple answer to the question of how to organize. Those are the ones with which the writer must truly wrestle, considering the piece-to-be one way, then another, writing an outline, then altering it. Changing the outline is much easier and quicker than altering the manuscript itself by rewriting and retyping it—one more good reason for making an outline.

However, the writer who studies how published features and articles are put together will likely discover that to the problem of organization there are several solutions that, like patent medicine, can be safely and effectively applied in many ordinary cases.

CHRONOLOGICAL. The chronological order of presentation works best with continuous narrative and with pieces that use the interview itself as the angle. In the following example from the *Independent Florida Alligator,* Dave Hogerty opens with a one-sentence lead followed by a two-sentence justifier in the same paragraph, then follows that with exposition and quotes to provide background, and then returns to the action. Hogerty's chronological construction is a little different than the usual, for he interrupts the narrative with out-of-the-context-of-the-action quotes that explain or show the subject's feelings. Such a technique can be a bad idea, but in this feature that won for its author a first-place award in the William Randolph Hearst Foundation's national collegiate writing competition, it worked.

As the characteristic rattle and squeak of the convenience store door broke the early-morning silence, Dan Eifert looked up from behind the counter to see two men entering the store. Moments later, Eifert would be lying on the floor with blood oozing from a bullet wound in his chest. His nighttime job at the neighborhood Majik Market would be over.

Friends and relatives had warned Eifert about the danger when he accepted his job, but the convenience store at 13th Street and 16th Avenue offered the only job within walking distance of his Cin City apartment, and the graveyard shift, from 11 p.m. to 7 a.m., was the only one that didn't conflict with his class schedule at the University of Florida.

Eifert was now 20 years old. He had been away from his home in Maitland for three years, ever since he left for the university, and he was determined to make his own decisions and support himself as he pursued a degree in mechanical engineering.

Eifert knew the risk involved in the job. The frequency of convenience store robberies was high, averaging one a week in Gainesville, but he wanted the independence and he tried to manage the fear. He told himself a friendly attitude could eliminate a lot of the danger.

"Before I actually worked, I had two days of training," Eifert said.

"The instructor talked about the possibility of being robbed and said if you were polite and cooperative, the robber would usually leave peacefully.

"I believed that was true. I also thought a friendly attitude would build a loyal clientele for the store."

Through such an approach, Eifert developed casual friendships with regulars, like the guy with the orange Toyota who came in every few days to buy chewing tobacco, and the girl who at first was angry, but later thankful that Eifert refused to sell her cigarettes — she never smoked again.

Eifert had been working for eight months, and the job was beginning to take its toll. The $105 a week satisfied his financial needs, but the pressure of school and lack of sleep were forcing him into depression.

"Near the end, school wasn't going too well," Eifert said. "On my last night, the biggest thing on my mind was deciding which of my four classes to drop."

Until the two men entered the store, the night of May 1, 1981 wasn't much different from most others. A lot of the regulars had been by earlier and the nightly 2 a.m. rush for a last six-pack of beer or bottle of wine had just ended. An Alachua County ordinance prohibits the sale of alcoholic beverages after 2 a.m.

In the night's line for liquor had been an old high school friend of Eifert who didn't have Friday class and was out on the town with a couple of friends.

"Terry Dunigan is a real jokester," Eifert said. "As she was going out the door, she stuck her head back in and yelled, 'Oh yeah, don't get robbed!' "

Eifert assured her he wouldn't.

Later that night he would be proved wrong, and with it, his philosophy of polite cooperation, blasted by a .38-caliber revolver.

"It was close to three," Eifert said. "I had just finished cleaning up and was working on a differential equation when the two men came in. Being black and about the same age, I assumed they were together.

"I got a little suspicious when the big guy went to the far aisle and seemed to just be wasting time while the smaller man came towards the counter."

Eifert greeted the small man as he would any strange customer.

"Hello, can I help you with something?" he asked while establishing eye contact.

"You can get a good idea of what kind of person you're dealing with by the look in his eye," Eifert explained.

"Give me all the receipts," the small man said, the words coming through his teeth in a low voice.

Eifert couldn't figure out why he would want the receipts. Then he saw the gun in the man's right hand and knew he meant the money.

"My knees and voice were shaking when I asked whether or not to include the change," Eifert said. "But I was still fairly calm, because the pistol was still at the man's side.

"I grabbed a paper bag and began filling it with bills, still believing that if I cooperated and gave him what he wanted, he'd just take the money and leave."

As the small man grabbed the bag with his left hand, he raised the gun and without warning fired a bullet into Eifert's chest.

"I was looking him straight in the eye and I had no idea he was going to shoot," Eifert said. "It all happened in a flash. The gun appeared as a blur and sounded like a firecracker.

"I felt no pain, but I did feel pressure where the bullet entered my chest. I took a step back out of surprise and put my hand over the hole.

"When I saw blood covering my arm and dripping off my elbow, I thought he had shot me in the heart."

Eifert was sure he was going to die as he dropped to one knee and slipped into a state of shock. The fleeing robber then fired a second shot, at the other man in the store, but missed him.

Eifert dragged himself out from behind the counter as he weakened and staggered across the store to the telephone.

He was struggling to remain conscious—which to him meant staying alive.

He reached for the receiver, but it slipped out of his bloody hand and dangled below his waist. He groped to retrieve it, then began to dial the 911 emergency number. Suddenly the big man was beside him.

The man was Harold Batie, a Gainesville fireman. As Eifert fell into his arms, Batie could see Eifert's face was turning chalky white and his lips blue. Batie took the phone and completed the emergency call.

Eifert lay back on the floor as the warm blood flowing from his chest formed a crimson pool around him and he began to lose perception of time. His mind seemed removed from his body as he observed the chaotic scene in the store.

"I heard the stern voice of a policeman ordering people away and I noticed the ambulance crew coming towards me," Eifert said.

The ambulance attendants were the same two who had stopped at the store earlier for Coke and lemonade, but now, instead of offering friendly conversation, they were shoving tubes and needles into Eifert's body in an effort to save him.

Eifert was now so shocked that he didn't realize the seriousness of his condition. He protested when one of the crew was about to cut off his favorite Firebird T-shirt. It had been given to him as a gift when he sold his car, a

Firebird. The attendant assured him there was a hole in the front of the shirt and it was stained with blood anyway.

Eifert felt relieved that the attendants had familiar faces, but while police were clearing out the crowd, Eifert's blood pressure dropped to 60 over zero – dangerously low. A body tourniquet had been applied and a saline solution was being forced through his body to keep his heart functioning.

The one thing Eifert still had a firm grasp on was the pain. It hadn't been immediate, but it was now worse than any he had ever experienced. "I've never felt pain like when they picked me up and put me on the stretcher board," he said.

En route to the hospital, Eifert became reacquainted with reality.

"I wasn't worried." he said. "But when the attendant reached up and pumped the saline bag, I felt wetness on my right side. At first I was confused, but then I realized the saline was coming out of the wound. It was then that I realized I was still in trouble.

"Things have made me happy and ecstatic before, but nothing has been more joyous than when I was finally at Shands (Teaching Hospital) and the doctor said they were going to put me under for surgery."

When he awoke at 7:30 that morning – the time he would normally leave work – Eifert was in the intensive care unit, where he remained in serious condition the next three days.

Two days after leaving intensive care, he went back into surgery to have the bullet removed. Eifert thought the bullet had passed through his body, but it had actually pierced the left lung and lodged against a rib in his back.

After a week's stay in the hospital and physical therapy to rebuild the muscles in his chest, Eifert's body recovered.

But his encounter with death had more permanent effects on other parts of his life. Now he realized that the concern expressed by his friends and relatives when he took the job was more than justified.

The store continued to pay his salary while Eifert was in the hospital, and worker's compensation took care of the medical expenses, but Eifert gave up the idea of ever going back to work at the store.

"Now I have more time to enjoy myself," he said.

"The biggest change I've experienced since the shooting is that I put a lot less emphasis on school. I probably still study more than most of my friends, but now I consider everything personal as more important."

Eifert felt a personal duty to testify for the prosecution in the trial of the man arrested and charged with the robbery and shooting. His name was Robert Lee Reed, 28, previously arrested 21 times on 29 charges, ranging from burglary to aggravated assault.

"I don't hate the man," Eifert said. "But I do think he's sick and I owed it to the person who's now working the graveyard shift to get him off the street."

In the trial, four months after the shooting, Eifert stood before the jury and described how the defendant had shot him. He opened his shirt and showed the jurors the bullet wound and the ten-inch surgical scar across his chest.

The verdict came within an hour.

Robert Lee Reed was found guilty and immediately sentenced to 75 years for armed robbery and two consecutive 30-year terms for two counts of attempted murder in the first degree.

Out of curiosity, Eifert went back to the store shortly after he was released from the hospital. From behind the counter where he once had stood, his replacement, a thin blonde who was also a UF student, spoke to him.

The girl noticed he was looking at the stain on the carpet behind the counter.

"One of the guys who works here says that's blood," the girl said. "Supposedly a clerk was shot here recently."

"And what do you think?" Dan asked.

"I think it's probably Coke or something," she answered.

Eifert hesitated, then looked the new clerk in the eye, wondering if she too might be trying to handle the fear of the job.

He smiled back and said, "Yeah you're probably right."

ALL SIDES. This type of organization usually works with pieces that are not only multi-source pieces but that must present different perspectives on the subject. The piece is divided into segments according to individual sources or different points of view. The writer may build a transitional phrase or sentence into the first paragraph following the end of each segment or move from one segment to the next without transitional phrases or sentences. In the following example, another article from Gainesville, Florida, published in *G., The Magazine of Gainesville,* author Aura Bland made a deliberate, clean break between segments, using a graphic device – asterisks – to let the reader know the piece was shifting into another part of the story. A line of white space or other device could be used to achieve the same effect.

Without street lights, S.W. Seventh Street looked pitch black except for a single light bulb on one of the porch ceilings that shone like a spotlight on the name "St. Francis House." The sign was carefully printed in white letters on a navy blue wooden board and nailed perfectly straight beside a screen door. Because of its neatness, it appeared out of place on the peeling house with broken cement steps, chipped brick pillars and dirt lawn.

Inside, another bare light bulb reflected off the dirty-white walls, filling the room with rays of white light. Various pieces of art deco tables and chairs, torn remnants of the mid-1960s, were pushed against the walls of the sitting room. In the center of the room, facing the fireplace, three matching easy chairs covered with thin, pea-green bedspreads circled a nonexistent fire.

A man sat on the couch holding a bowl of macaroni and beef a few inches from his chin. In between spoonfuls, he said his name was Joe McDole and he was 41 years old – he looked 15 years older. His smile revealed a single yellow tooth on the upper left side of his mouth, and his voice sounded like an old man's when he talked. Gray stubble covered his chin and cheeks, and his hair was still wet from his shower.

A young woman wearing tight, cut-off shorts and a T-shirt walked out of the kitchen and sat on the arm of one of the green chairs. She had long, frizzy, black hair, warm brown eyes and a clear complexion. When she smiled, she showed two rows of brown, crooked teeth.

A tall, dark-haired man with a belly that hung over his belt, straining the buttons of his shirt, followed her out of the kitchen and asked her for a cigarette. She handed him the pack she had been holding loosely in her hand, and he shook one out. He said he was staying at St. Francis House because the operation he was supposed to have at the Veterans Administration Hospital was cancelled and he didn't have the money to pay for a place to sleep.

St. Francis House, like the other emergency shelters in town, the Salvation Army and Bread of Life (now called World Ministry Outreach) tend to draw transients to Gainesville. Since it is a college town, the first sizable city off of I-75 after a traveler crosses the state line, and has a large V.A. Hospital offering free health care to veterans, Gainesville has become especially attractive to out-ot-work, penniless travelers.

Joe McDole, scraping the bowl and putting it down on the hexagon-shaped table beside him, said, "Gainesville is just like a big city, because it has places you can go and stay for free, and people know that 300 miles from here."

"It's called a pipeline," Dennis Kipp, the pot-bellied veteran, said. "You can go down the road and you run into a guy drinking coffee somewhere, and he'll say, 'If you go to Gainesville, go to St. Francis House and they'll put you up.'"

St. Francis House provides a bed for about 50 such people a month, each of whom usually stay three days, sometimes longer. Bread of Life sleeps 80 to 100 people a month. The Salvation Army does not have a monthly average, but they provided 255 lodgings and served 997 meals during December; and in January, they served 1466 meals and provided 566 lodgings.

Because the shelters limit the number of days a person can stay, some people move from shelter to shelter and are counted more than once. These figures include Gainesville residents with emergency needs as well as transients.

Free bag lunches, which before January were given out at St. Francis Hall on the corner of N.W. 1st Avenue and 17th Street, are given out at lunch time in front of St. Francis House at 24 S.W. Seventh Street, because the St. Francis board of directors want to provide food and lodging at one location. Through the free lunch program, St. Francis gives out as many as 60 bag lunches a day, Sister Claire, president of the free lunch service, said. That's approximately 22,000 a year.

***

Benny and Carol Ayers sat on their backpacks on the lawn in front of St. Francis Hall, finishing a free peanut butter sandwich and doughnut that made up their free lunch. Benny was 35 years old with small, slanted eyes, a bristly mustache and thin, scraggly hair that brushed against his shoulders. Carol, 39, had a smooth young face and silky dark hair pulled back in a gold barrette and tied with a pink ribbon. Both wore faded blue jeans, hers with a ring of damp dirt around the hem, where they brushed the ground when she walked.

The Ayerses, who were just passing through, wandered into Gainesville from I-75 "to see what was going on," Benny said. The truck driver with whom they had hitched a ride, had dropped them off in front of St. Francis Hall, where he told them they could get a free lunch.

"You talk; I'm eating," Carol Ayers said, pointing to her husband and scraping the doughnut's powdered sugar off her mouth with the back of her hand.

"We got into town about an hour ago. We just happened to get a ride here," Benny said. "I worked in a furniture plant in Roanoke, Virginia, and got laid off. Things aren't going too good.

"We're gonna stop at the Plasma Center and then go back on the road. Don't look like there's much work here. Too many people around like this," Benny said, his slanted eyes skimming over the ten or so people lounging around St. Francis Hall.

He said he and his wife had been on the road for six days and would have made it to Florida sooner if their car hadn't broken down outside of Savannah.

"We left the car on the side of the road, took what we could and put it on our back," Benny said.

He stood and slowly lifted the green backpack onto his back and, leaning forward, he pulled at the straps to get it balanced. Then he picked up the other backpack and held if for Carol while she put her arms through the straps.

"We don't know where we're going," Benny said. "We're just looking for work." They walked away, down 17th

Street, then turned left on University Avenue, heading for the Plasma Center.

***

City Commissioner Mark Goldstein views the free lunch program as a problem because it encourages vagrants to hang around inner-city neighborhoods. He also says vagrants are attracted to the university town because "students are easy prey to those who want to rip them off."

"My observations suggest that Gainesville is increasingly seen by vagrants as an easy Southern town to exploit," he said. "A place with vulnerable citizens and gullible students. In my opinion it is time to hassle back. Our officers need to roust them out aggressively and repeatedly."

But others, like the people at St. Francis House, supported by Gainesville churches, want to help vagrants by providing a few nights shelter.

"We're not a flophouse," Bob Tansig, a young volunteer worker and member of St. Francis board of directors, said. "We're trying to help people get established."

Everyone who stays at St. Francis House must first get a police clearance. He or she must show identification at the police station, where a computer check makes sure he doesn't have a record or is not wanted by the police. Guests are not allowed to drink and if they come in drunk or smelling of alcohol, they are immediately asked to leave. The guests must leave the house by eight in the morning and they cannot return until five that afternoon. And if they're not back by 10 p.m., they are asked to leave.

"We'll give them a few days or maybe a week to find a job, get a pay check and find their own place," Tansig said. "Then they're on their own. After they've stayed once, they can't come back. If they want to stay in Gainesville, they have to make other arrangements."

***

The Hale family stayed at St. Francis House for four days. There were six members of the family – the middle-aged mother and stepfather, their 16-year-old son, Clint, their nine-year-old son, Kevin, their daughter, Vickie Lee Hale, a 19-year-old single mother of a three-week old baby.

After the third night, Tansig asked the Hales to make other sleeping arrangements because the parents had not returned by 10 p.m. But the next night, another volunteer worker was on duty, and the Hales came back, deposited the children at the house and went out for the evening. When Tansig came on duty that night, he let the children stay because, he said, he didn't have the heart to put the baby out on the streets.

That night, Vickie Lee sat on the bed, bathing the birdlike legs of her red, baby daughter. Vickie, her face spotted with pimples, had shoulder-length hair and white, even teeth. Her black mascara was smeared underneath her eyes, and her bare feet were black with dirt.

"My stepdad's a roofer, and we left Texas because it got too cold for him to work. It was two degrees below at noontime, so we decided to come to Florida, where it's warmer," she said, trying with difficulty to wrap a thin, cloth diaper around the tiny baby's bottom.

It had taken the Hales three days to get to Gainesville from Amarillo, Texas. They had left Texas with $110, some clothes and food in a red Toyota pickup truck with a handmade wooden camper on the back. Clint and Kevin rode lying down in the camper and Vickie, her baby, Tanya, and parents rode in the front seat.

"We only made it halfway because we ran out of gas and money," Vickie said. "So we stopped at a church where we were given a box of food and enough gas money to make it to Gainesville."

***

Mary Jean Baughman, director of Gainesville Community Ministry, Inc., a private Christian agency funded by area churches to help people with emergency needs, said some people really know how to use emergency services to their advantage.

"People will leave someplace with nothing and plan to travel across the country by stopping at agency after agency for food and gas money. And they make it," Baughman said. "A man who came in to see me for help told me he and his family had traveled from the Virgin Islands to Fort Lauderdale with plane and bus tickets given to them by different churches. Then he proceeded to tell me he didn't accept charity."

Gainesville Community Ministry helps as many as 200 individuals a month, half Gainesville residents, half transients. The agency was formed to avoid duplication of services because people would go from one Gainesville church to another, getting help from each one. GCM gives out bag lunches after 1:30 p.m. when the free lunch service at St. Francis House closes. The agency also gives out groceries, gasoline assistance, utility and rent loans, medicine assistance, baby-care items, and refers individuals to other agencies that can best help their needs. Applicants are thoroughly screened, and their needs carefully assessed.

A 59-year-old man in a thin, plaid sports jacket, too big in the shoulders and too short in the sleeves, walked into the red brick building, GCM's headquarters, located at 508 S.W. 2nd Avenue, holding a crumpled cloth hat in both hands. He asked Baughman if there was any chance he could get a pair of glasses.

STRING OF PEARLS. This type of organization will often work when a piece must offer several examples of the subject it is presenting to the reader. It simply places them one after another, letting the reader see one, then another, then another. The following example of this type, published in *Historic Preservation* magazine, was Part II of a series by Caskie Stinnett. The piece moved immediately to the first pearl, with a descriptive lead but little or no justifier.

[First pearl]

A FEW MILES north of Gloucester, on Massachusetts' rocky Cape Ann peninsula, lies Rockport, a sleepy sea town that has steadfastly refused to abandon its old rituals and way of life despite the fact that it is situated squarely in the tourist corridor extending from Boston north to Newburyport. Rockport possesses style, the inextinguishable style of an ancient seaport that knew prosperity during the days of sailing ships and which stubbornly refuses to lower its standards to accommodate a more informal and materialistic age. There is to the village an atmosphere of ingratiating stateliness, a stateliness that is nowhere more pronounced than at Seacrest Manor, a bed and breakfast inn that so perfectly fits the town that one can't imagine it existing anywhere else.

A spacious inn, although it contains only eight guest rooms, Seacrest Manor faces the ocean on Marmion Way, where it seems spiritually as well as physically linked to the sea. From the sun deck on a clear day guests can see Kittery, Maine, nearly 40 miles away.

And unless a fog sweeps in from the North Atlantic, which happens occasionally, the twin lighthouses of Thachers Island are always in view.

Dwight MacCormack, Jr., who with Leighton Saville reactivated the inn in 1973, feels that Seacrest Manor is a living part of Rockport and that the town would be culturally poorer without it.

"I think the inn matches the village, which is as it should be," MacCormack said recently. The inn had been built in the early years of the 20th century as a private home, but it was already licensed as a guest house when it was acquired by MacCormack, the resident manager, and Saville, an NBC executive. While Seacrest Manor provides a panoramic view of the sea, it is surrounded by more than two acres of garden and woodland.

The appeal of a bed and breakfast inn first struck MacCormack when he was living in England. "I became used to the concept when I was staying in Kent," he explained. "I was there for a year and enjoyed it, but I was suddently struck by the thought that it was time to go on to another occupation." When he returned to the United States, he became involved in Seacrest Manor after a stint as a college teacher.

Breakfasts are of enormous importance to an inn of this kind, MacCormack believes, and he and his partner go to great lengths to provide extraordinary ones. He was greatly pleased when in 1980 *Town and Country* included Seacrest Manor in an article on "Great American Breakfasts."

"An innkeeper can't offer his guests a continental breakfast and still call it a bed and breakfast inn," MacCormack asserts firmly. "The breakfast is important to the concept and category. Aside from the standard breakfast items such as fresh fruit, eggs, bacon, toast and coffee, we go out of the way to create specialities, things such as Irish oatmeal with chopped dates, corn fritters or blueberry-buttermilk pancakes," Breakfast, of course, is included in the room rate—the test of a true bed and breakfast inn.

Afternoon tea is served in the living room, while guests who wish may settle down and read in large leather chairs beside the fireplace in the library. An atmosphere of relaxation prevails, preserved by the inn's minimum guest age of 16. "We're selling peace and quiet," said Saville. The guest rooms are carpeted and hand-

somely furnished, some with antiques picked up in the Cape Ann area. "Nothing structurally has been added or changed recently," MacCormack said. "We are located in a residential area that has very severe restrictions as to what can be done. However, changes in interior decoration are made constantly."

Operating a bed and breakfast inn, even one as modest in size as Seacrest Manor, involves long hours, MacCormack has discovered, and for that reason the inn is open only 11 months a year. Every January the inn is at rest. When asked what he does during January, the innkeeper replied: "I go to New York City and collapse."

The slight difference between a bed and breakfast inn and a small hotel all but disappears in the definition, yet there is a difference. The bed and breakfast inn, so common in the British Isles, as MacCormack discovered, possesses an informality, a home-like quality, that hotels almost invariably lack. The owner usually lives there; one suspects that this is his home, too. An old English proverb holds that "getting out of the inn is half the journey." This is a tribute to the comfort of the bed and breakfast inn; the guest is inclined to tarry.

There is no hurry to resume the journey. Unlike the sterile and uniform motel, where tonight's lodging is so similar to last night's that one wonders if one has moved at all, the inn is a pleasant part of the trip, a restful respite that in itself is something to be savored and enjoyed.

I once stayed in a small English inn in West Riding, in Yorkshire, and I will never forget it, although its name has long disappeared from my memory. It was autumn, and I awoke early and took a walk down a country lane. A mist hung over the brook, the air was crisp, and a hint of wood smoke drifted to me from some undisclosed source. I went back to the inn, ate breakfast ravenously, and went on my way. I have forgotten now where I was going, but the memory of that inn stays stubbornly with me.

But if the bed and breakfast inn is a part of our English heritage, it is a welcome one in an era of turnpikes and interstate highways, of motels, of computerized check-ins and of franchised fast-food restaurants. The inn is the shunpiker's discovery. It lies always on a smaller road or in a village, and it is a prize for those who have no interest in boasting of the distance covered in a single day. Here, in a sunny garden, you can sample a fine wine while the scent of something cooking curls out of the kitchen. The tables of the inn are often set under fruit trees dappled with sunlight; or they are pulled beside a cozy fire, the snow banked against a windowpane; or they nestle against a window overlooking the sea, as was the case at Seacrest Manor.

[Second pearl]

I spent a winter's night recently at Stonehurst Manor, a large graceful inn set in a pine forest near North Conway, N.H. The Mt. Washington Valley is popular with skiers, but there was no bustle of skiers clomping through the inn eager to get to the slopes at the first light of day. No, there was an imposing silence that spoke of rest and luxury and slumber. Stonehurst Manor was originally built in 1872 as the summer home of the Bigelow family, which founded the Bigelow Carpet Company. Destroyed by fire three years later, it was rebuilt the following year. After several transformations, the great manor was converted into an inn during the 1940s, and it has remained a public house ever since.

It was snowing fitfully when I came downstairs before dinner. The lobby was bright and cheerful. At one side of an enormous fireplace, in which logs were blazing, there was a small bar; across the room were rounded window seats upholstered in bright red corduroy. Above the fireplace was a heavy oak mantel and oak paneling, while lighted Victorian sconces on the walls and heavy rugs added to the general feeling of richness and grace from another era.

After a drink I went to one of the three dining rooms where, seated in a fan-back wicker chair at a candle-lit table, I had dinner. While the quality of the food may not have been what the Guide Michelin would have described as *mérite un détour,* or worth a detour, it was extraordinarily good for an inn and was served faultlessly. The menu ran heavily to veal dishes – there were 10 of them – but after *crudités* served with dill seed, I chose rack of lamb and wild rice. The lamb was tender, the rice well cooked. For dessert there was Black Forest cake, which seemed appropriate for the place, as well as pecan pie and a Grand Marnier cake. After dinner, I wandered back to the fireplace, where I had a brandy before going to bed.

At breakfast the next morning I was seated in another dining room and was surprised to find behind me a leaded stained-glass window. There were a number of these lovely windows in the building, I was told by a waiter. Stonehurst Manor seemed determined to send its visitors on their way well fed. Breakfast was hearty; I had sausage and eggs, fresh orange juice, hot muffins and coffee. The breakfast room filled early, and like me, most of the guests seemed to be on their way to some other destination. They had chosen an inn over the string of motels on the town's main street because they preferred the gracious atmosphere that it offered. If I go back to the White Mountains of New Hampshire, I shall certainly go back to Stonehurst Manor.

New England perhaps has more bed and breakfast inns than any other section of the country, but I have no idea why this is true. Presumably it is a vestige of the region's colonial past. New England clings stubbornly to tradition; here custom has the strength of anchor chain. The Village Inn at Yarmouth Port, on Cape Cod, was once the home of a sea captain, while the Old Yarmouth Inn, in the same village, offers guests not only breakfast but also the chance to look at the guest register of the inn covering the years from 1866 to 1869. The book was discovered behind a wallboard when the building was restored in 1971.

New England inns vary greatly in size, from the Chetwynd House in Kennebunkport, Maine, with only four guest rooms, to the famous Old Tavern at Grafton, Vt., where Henry David Thoreau, Gen. U.S. Grant, Theodore Roosevelt and Oliver Wendell Holmes were, at one time or another, occupants of the inn's 35 rooms and five cottages.

[Third pearl]

One of the oldest inns still in operation is the Black Bass, on the Delaware River in Bucks County, Pennsylvania. Perched on the edge of the ancient canal beside the river, the inn dates back to the 1700s, when a stagecoach route followed the river westward toward the Delaware Water Gap.

Built of thick fieldstone, as were many period buildings hereabouts, the inn has eight guest rooms and three suites, all furnished with antiques and each named for some historical place or figure—who may or may not have stayed there; the records long ago disappeared.

But it is a fact that Adlai Stevenson found the place very much to his taste, and such show-business figures as Ann-Margaret, Angela Lansbury and Mabel Mercer discovered the inn when they were appearing at the summer theater in nearby New Hope. I spent a weekend once in the General Grant Room, an immense ornate chamber with high ceilings, massive exposed beams and a magnificent view of the fast-flowing river. I initially felt that I was occupying a room in a museum, but I grew to like it and felt quite at home there when I left.

The Black Bass Inn has been altered somewhat over the years, but the basic structure is intact. Owner Herbert Ward is fiercely protective of the old building and reluctant to make any changes. In most of the downstairs public rooms there are stone fireplaces. A long verandah that faces the river has, over the years, been glassed in for the winter months and now serves as the main dining room, and in summer and on weekends it is invariably crowded. There are other, smaller dining rooms on the first floor, and a small but cheerful bar. In the winter there is always a fire in the entrance lobby, and guests are welcome to have a drink beside the fire. But an atmosphere of informality prevails, and visitors are left to do what they wish.

Since the inn is fairly isolated in the country, there is not a great deal to do other than explore the countryside or drive into New Hope or Lambertville, both about a half-hour's drive down the river. I crossed the footbridge that spans the river at the inn and took a long walk down the New Jersey side, returning at dusk when some of the first guests began arriving from New Hope and Philadephia for dinner.

The tables were candle-lit and the food good—not excellent but good. I retired early to sink into a deep mattress and instant slumber. There may have been traffic noises, since the inn sits on the very edge of the road—a local road, not a busy highway—but I didn't hear them. I did hear the muted whisper of the river, and it speeded the arrival of sleep. A continental breakfast was at my door when I awoke the next morning, and I ate it at a table beside the window.

Since the Black Bass has a reputation for resembling a French or English inn, a great many foreign guests seek it out. "One day I had a telephone call from Sydney, Australia, and one from Paris," Hubert Ward told me. "I don't know how word gets around, but I suppose it all starts with contented guests." He's right, of course.

[Fourth pearl]

While it doesn't appear in many guidebooks of inns in New England, the Phoenix, on Gibson Avenue in Narragansett, is close enough to serve as

an overnight base for visits to New-
port's great homes. Originally, the inn
was a handsome Stanford White-de-
signed mansion built in the late 19th
century by Louis Sherry, founder of the
restaurant and confectionary business.
The house was largely destroyed by
fire a few years after it was completed,
but it was rebuilt and 10 years ago was
taken over by a couple named Joyce
and David Peterson. There are five
guest bedrooms, all handsomely
furnished, a large living room where
guests enjoy tea by the fireplace, and a
formal dining room where breakfast is
served.

STEP BY STEP. This type of organization is usually reserved for how-to
pieces, as in this example from an article in *Reader's Digest,* written by
John Wolfe.

W HEN SOMEONE ASKS you
to deliver a talk in front of a
group, what's your reaction?
If you're like most people, it's sheer ter-
ror. According to *The Book of Lists,* the
No. 1 phobia in America is the fear of
public speaking.

That's unfortunate, for "public
speaking" does not necessarily imply –
or require – a mass audience. "We have
more than 100,000 members throughout the world," says Terry McCann, executive director of Toastmasters International, "and most of them don't
aspire to greatness on the platform.
Their problem, generally, is in talking
to groups of five or ten people. A business executive, a supervisor in a fac-
tory, a section-worker in an office – all
can increase their effectiveness
through better public speaking. The
opportunities are limitless."

Can *you* improve your speaking
skill? Of course! Anyone can. All you
have to do is learn how.

The two steps in making any
speech – preparation and delivery – are
equally important. Here are four rules
for planning your talk:

1) Pick the right subject. It should be
a topic about which you have strong
feelings. The only way to be comfortable in front of an audience is to know
what you're talking about – and to believe in what you're trying to get
across. While our American hostages
were being held in Iran, many of their
wives appeared on national television.
Even without formal training, these
women spoke with true eloquence.
Their pleas came from the heart.

Choose a subject of direct interest
to your listeners and slant your message to them. Assume that you've
come up with an idea to improve office
efficiency. If you're called upon to sell
your proposal to the board of directors,
emphasize the profits it will bring;
when presenting the plan to the people
who will implement it, stress how it
will make their jobs easier. Everyone
wants to know: What's in it for me?

2) Organize your points logically. You
need a beginning – usually a brief
description of the problem you intend
to attack; a middle that enumerates the
main points in your solution; and an end
that summarizes your entire presentation. An old rule for speakers puts it
this way: "Tell them what you're going
to tell them; then tell them; and, finally,
tell them what you've told them."

It also helps to put "hooks" on each
major point. Many of us were taught to
memorize the names of the Great
Lakes by remembering the mnemonic
H-O-M-E-S – standing for *H*uron, *O*n-
tario, *M*ichigan, *E*rie and *S*uperior.
Mnemonics help your listeners follow
your train of thought. They make your
message more memorable. And they
help you remember what you want to
say.

3) Rehearse in private. After you've
planned your presentation, you need to
practice delivering it. It's best to do
this in private, not in front of a friend
or spouse. You're rehearsing a speech

to a group, not a one-on-one discussion. Try to visualize the audience. "See" and "hear" the positive responses you'll be receiving.

Whenever possible, do a final review in the room where you'll be speaking. This way, you will feel at home during your actual performance.

4) *Keep notes to a minimum.* The worst thing to do is try to read your speech. It's virtually impossible to make a reading sound spontaneous. If necessary, list your major headings on index cards—with only a few words on each card. A quick glance will trigger your thoughts. The less you refer to notes, the better you'll communicate with your audience. Public speaking is essentially a matter of communication between you and your audience. For most speakers, copious notes are more of a hindrance than a help.

LIST. This type is one of the simplest ways to organize and write the piece. The writer simply categorizes the material, writes a lead, then presents the parts of the piece, each part with its own identifying and introductory subhead, as in this article on the 1985 car models, written by Ellis Sandoz III and published in *Baton Rouge Magazine.*

FOR 1985's automotive offerings, car-makers have generally responded to the public's call for trim looks without a wimpy constitution by, on one hand, lightening and tightening and, on the other, by turbo charging and fuel injecting. European-style aerodynamics have been incorporated for efficiency and good looks, while plain old American ponies have been harnessed under the hood for the new Main Street pink slip crowd.

The pages that follow provide a glimpse of what to expect from car-makers with area outlets. Keep in mind that this review is not intended to be comprehensive nor overly technical in its treatment of makes or models.

Cadillac

The introduction of the 1985 front-drive Sedan and Coupe DeVilles marks the end of the large rear-drive models of the venerable line. The Fleetwood Brougham will, however, be continued as a rear-drive model in unchanged two-door and four-door forms.

The new DeVilles, actually introduced last April, introduce such amenities as a standard six-way power seat on the driver's side (optional for passenger), power windows that operate up to 10 minutes after the ignition is turned off, a stereo radio with signal-seeking scanner and digital display, electronic climate control, and a fuel data center, which includes display of instantaneous and average fuel economy, estimated driving range, and fuel used.

All other Cadillac models are said to be unchanged from '84s, with the exception of Cimarron, which will feature new front styling and new-look alloy wheels.

Chevrolet

Increased performance emphasis and a General Motors entry into the mini-van wars highlight the 1985 model year for Chevrolet. Also, two new Japanese imports will join Chevette at the bottom of the price ladder. While the Sprint will certainly not be available in this area in 1985, the Isuzu-supplied Spectrum probably will reach this market. The Spectrum is a front wheel drive model to be offered in both two-door hatchback and four-door notchback styles.

Visual changes will be minimal throughout the Chevrolet line, with a sports package available on J-cars and a snazzy high performance, dressed up "IROC-Z" package available in Z28 Camaros. The main difference in current Chevies will be larger, more powerful engines.

The Astro mini-van will be available in late October as either a cargo or passenger model, seating up to eight persons. Astro is 176.8 inches in length, 71 inches high, and 77 inches wide. It can carry a 1,700-pound payload in its 151.6-cubic feet of cargo volume, and has a trailer towing capacity of 5,000 pounds.

Subaru

Details are sketchy due to the secretive nature of this Japanese manufacturer, but the '85 Subarus are expected to take on a whole new look. Redesigned "sheet metal" (a term used by dealers and salespeople to denote outward body shaping) for a more futuristic and aerodynamic form, hidden headlight options, and longer wheelbases are some of the features to look for across the line.

Subaru is also expected to unveil its new two-passenger commuter car, which will get approximately 62 miles per gallon in the city. The car will probably cost in the neighborhood of $5,000 and will have a top speed of about 55 m.p.h.

Volvo

Volvo fans will be glad to know that a new line — the 740 series — will appear during the 1985 model year. This line will take its shape from the current top-of-the-line 760 series, which has a sleek . . . .

Q&A. Although the Q&A, in which the writer asks a question and the subject answers it, is more like a transcript than a written article or feature, it does work sometimes, usually when the subject is a celebrity or VIP. This excerpt from a piece on comedian Steve Martin, written by Ben Fong-Torres and published in *Rolling Stone,* is an example. The writer constructs a lead, then a justifier, then starts asking questions.

Offstage, with friends or strangers, Steve is, simply, off. He's a cooperative interview, but he doesn't want to talk about fellow comedians, he says, "because all I'm gonna do is say nice things, and it's gonna be so boring." He wants to keep his relationship with Bernadette Peters (costar of 'Pennies') private. And the same goes for his art collection. Agonizing over whether to even talk about it, he explains: "As a comedian, I'm willing to trade out my private thoughts about things that are personal to me for space in the magazine, and I'm willing to say dumb things that, six months later, I go, 'Why did I say that?' But when it comes to art, which is so personal—and I am not trying to make it part of my personality—I'm not willing to say dumb things about it. I want the freedom to be stupid about it, to learn about it, to think about something I still don't understand. It's like why I'm a vegetarian, I don't know. I can't defend myself, and I don't have to defend myself. It's like the artist doesn't *have to explain or justify anything about it. And I think it's important for me to keep that position, for my own personal health."*

But on occasion, Martin the comedian emerges. He notices my scribbling into a notebook. "What're you writing down?" he asks.

I tell him, "Striped dress shirt, black slacks . . . ."

"Well," he volunteers, "my shoes are mauve. They're dress shoes, but I want to break them in, so I'm wearing them two hours a day." He chuckles.

And the socks?

"Oh, I'm breaking in these socks, too."

Why did you decide to take such a risk with your career?

I was asked about that before I went into the project, and there was no hesitation. When I first started doing my act, it was not . . . normal. It was not what was expected. That's why the public caught onto it. And I said, "If I start getting trapped by my own sameness, I'm not doing what they secretly want, which is for me to do what I want to do."

The last time I saw you, you said this movie would be the biggest challenge of your life. Did your expectations come true?

More than I thought, I was in such a state. I'd been on the road–about seventeen years. But three years really steady, and it was debilitating. You get physically tired, emotionally tired, and start wondering what you're doing.

It got to the point where when I'd do new material, it sounded like old material even to *me [puzzled laugh]*.

Organizing Raw Material

Making an outline will not only organize the piece, it will organize the raw material of the piece as well. That mound of transcripts, clips, Xeroxes, tear sheets, p.r. handouts, and hand-written notes may be pulled apart, then sorted and categorized according to the numbers of the outline. The writer puts all the material that pertains to the lead, for example, in a pile with a "1" on top of it. All material from which the justifier will be written, he puts in a pile with a "2" on it. Material for the next chunk of the article is in another pile with a "3" on it, and so on.

Sorting the material that way will require going through the material once to categorize it, then only once more when the piece is actually being written. It avoids the ordeal of reading through all the material repeatedly, looking for whatever bit of information is needed, and thereby saves time and reduces the risk of repetition in the article. Such a system is especially important and helpful when writing a piece of 3,000 words or more, with many sources.

Some material, of course, will include information for more than one chunk of the piece. A page of the transcript, for example, might include documentation needed for the justifier, a set of quotes needed for section 3, and an anecdote for the conclusion. In that case, the writer simply marks the outline-section numbers on the material itself, in the margins, indicating which sentences or paragraphs are for which section–2, 3, and 8 in the outline, for example. He then places the material on pile 2. When part 2 of the piece has been written, he moves the material to pile 3, and when that part has been written, he moves the material to pile 8.

KEEPING TRACK OF WORDAGE. Most assigned pieces are assigned at a certain length: 1,500 words, 2,500 words, etc. Even if an editor has not specified length, the publication probably has a policy about it, and submitted pieces that exceed that length limit by a substantial amount ordinarily have little chance for acceptance. You can examine issues of the publication to learn the normal length of the pieces it runs. A writer must consider length every time he or she writes.

If a finished piece is too long, it must be trimmed. Trimming is one more time-consuming step in producing the article or feature – and a waste of words and work. It is far better to write the piece to the expected or acceptable length, thus avoiding a piece that's much too short or much too long (the more common fault).

One good way to write to length is to assign percentages to the sections of the outline. The percentages are ordinarily dictated by the material and the angle, and the writer assigns them to the sections and writes them next to the section numbers on the outline. For example, the writer might decide the lead should be no more than 12 percent of the total piece, the justifier no more than 5 percent. The remaining 83 percent of the piece is to be divided among the various sections in the body of the piece and the conclusion. Then he determines how many words constitute 12 percent of the total piece; for example, if the piece is to be 3,000 words long, then the lead should not run more than about 360 words. The writer follows that same procedure with each section of the piece, so in actually writing the piece, he knows how many words to allot to each chunk. If one chunk turns out to need more words than planned, he can reduce the percentage of some other chunk or chunks, adjusting as the piece progresses.

Such a procedure will spare the writer the trouble of later trimming and cutting the finished piece and, more important, will eliminate the danger of having a piece rejected simply because it is too far over a publication's normal word limit.

TRANSITIONS. Transitions are not so much a matter of *what* the writer says in moving from one part of the piece to another; rather they are more a matter of *when* the writer says it. Transitions are a function of organization rather than of writing.

Pieces that are well organized prepare the reader for shifting from one chunk of information to the next. When the reader has finished one chunk, he is naturally ready to learn the next logical chunk. A smooth transitional phrase might help ease the reader's passage, but the writer should be able to get by with a simple introduction to the next section.

To see what I mean, go back and reread three earlier examples. See how simply and straightforwardly Terrie Riecke moved from one subsubject to the next in her garbage man piece, how Caskie Stinnett simply pulled the next pearl onto the string in his bed-and-breakfast piece, and how Aura Bland made transitions from asterisks in her hoboes piece.

The goal is to satisfy the reader's curiosity about one part of the story, then immediately turn his attention to the next logical part so naturally and effortlessly that he is barely conscious of the shift. Read through the previous examples to see how and how well those authors managed to achieve that effect.

CHAPTER NINE

The Conclusion

WHEN THE READER FINISHES a well-done feature or article, he should feel as satisfied as a diner does at the completion of a six-course dinner. For the diner, dessert, the final course, provides the one remaining element required to satisfy him. At the same moment it signals clearly the end of an enjoyable experience, so the diner pushes away from the table contented. For the reader, dessert is the conclusion, a special part of the piece drawn from the writer's material to fulfill the same purpose dessert does for the diner.

It shouldn't be necessary for a graphic device to tell the reader, "This is the end." The indication of the end should be a structural part of the piece itself, for which the writer is responsible, not the art director or editor. The conclusion and the effect it is intended to have on the reader, of course, will depend on the material, the nature of the piece, and the angle. The writer fashions a conclusion to fit a specific feature or article. However, there are several standard types of conclusions that usually work well, and the writer may choose one of them for a particular piece according to the effect desired and the material available.

Here are six such standard types of conclusions:

Rounded

The effect of a rounded conclusion is to return the reader to the spot where the writer met him in the lead. The writer does so by bringing into the conclusion the same (or similar) scene, action, character, or idea introduced in the lead. Writer Martha Abdella used a rounded conclusion in a piece on a used-furniture dealer, John Field.

The lead.

Outside the plain white building, two rocking chairs rocked in the wind while an old wooden nightstand and a used baby's crib sat next to each other in front of a large picture window. The words "Big Sale" were handwritten on a piece of paper taped to the window.

Inside, some of the articles for sale seemed to take on character and speak when people walked by them. A small yellow desk jumped into sight with a fluorescent green sign on it that said, "Look Mommy, only $25." The big chair with green-and-yellow-plaid fabric had a sign pinned to the arm: "Sit down, I'm comfy and cheap too."

Even the man sitting behind the oak desk smoking a cigarette had a sign on him. He got up and with a country drawl said, "How ya'll doin'? Can I help you with somethin'?" His sign was on his head. He wore an orange-and-blue baseball cap with the words "Plunder House Used Furn" in bold orange letters.

John Field, the man in the cap, . . .

After the article showed Field and gave the reader information about Field and the used-furniture business, author Abdella rounded it off with this conclusion:

Then, back in Gainesville, behind the plain white building, John can be seen unloading more furniture. The walls in Plunder House bulge as more sofas, mattresses, dining room sets and chairs are piled in. His business has grown so much that he opened up the wall to the room he used to rent for karate classes and John now uses it as part of his showroom.

When all the "new" used furniture is organized in the store, John, in his orange-and-blue baseball cap, relaxes behind his desk, props his feet up and drags on a cigarette. A customer walks in, and with his country drawl John once more says, "How ya'll doin'? What can I do for you today?"

In his feature about a convenience store clerk, Dan Eifert, who was shot during a holdup of the store, Dave Hogerty opened his story with a brief scene in the store, then after telling the victim's story in vivid detail chronologically, brought Eifert and the reader back to the scene of the crime.

The lead.

As the characteristic rattle and squeak of the convenience store door broke the early-morning silence, Dan Eifert looked up from behind the counter to see two men entering the store. Moments later, Eifert would be lying on the floor with blood oozing from a bullet wound in his chest. His nighttime job at the neighborhood Majik Market would be over.

The conclusion.

Out of curiosity, Eifert went back to the store shortly after he was released from the hospital. From behind the counter where he once had stood, his replacement, a thin blonde who was also a UF student, spoke to him.

The girl noticed he was looking at the stain on the carpet behind the counter.

"One of the guys who works here says that's blood," the girl said. "Supposedly a clerk was shot here recently."

"And what do you think?" Dan asked.

"I think it's probably Coke or something," she answered.

Eifert hesitated, then looked the new clerk in the eye, wondering if she too might be trying to handle the fear of the job.

He smiled back and said, "Yeah, you're probably right."

The rounded effect can also be achieved without an anecdote or re-creation of a scene, as writer Phil Keisling did in an article on how to save our public schools, published in *The New Republic.*

The lead.

In 1960, six-year-old Ruby Bridges braved the taunts of white racists to become one of the first blacks to enroll in an all-white school system. Two decades later, Bridges took her eldest child out of that same school system and placed him in a Catholic school. "I don't like to put down public schools," she said, "but my son wasn't really learning the way he should have."

As Bridges painfully discovered, integrating the public schools is only half the battle.

The conclusion.

Good public schools need not become an endangered species. But if we continue to ignore warning signals such as the Coleman report, it won't take a sociologist to perform a post-mortem. Parents like Ruby Bridges could easily explain what went wrong.

Summary

This type of conclusion offers the reader something that will sum up the message of the piece, hammering home the point. Here's an example of the type, written by Michael Goldberg for *Rolling Stone.* The piece is about musician Van Morrison, whom the author says is "one of the more mysterious stars of popular music." After presenting anecdotes and quotes showing Morrison's oddness in the body of the piece, author Goldberg ended with this conclusion:

I was sitting by Morrison's pool, thinking about our previous meeting, when the stillness was broken; the gate swung open and Morrison appeared. He seemed at ease, casually entering his yard. Then he noticed me and his body visibly tensed. I walked up to meet him.

"I tried to call you," he mumbled. He was not smiling. "Were you home?" We walked through the gate to the driveway where his silver-gray BMW was parked. "Well, I can't do it today," he announced. He stood there uncomfortably, peering at me through plastic-framed glasses. "Things just came up. I don't know. . . ." He shrugged. "Call me next week. Call me Monday," he said. "Uh, I hope this didn't inconvenience you."

I said I'd call on Monday. He nodded. I turned away and walked to my car. I looked back and Morrison and his BMW had vanished. That's the last I saw of Van Morrison.

"I've seen him change his mind five times in one hour," said a former business associate when I related the incident to him. "He's a funny guy."

Following is the summary conclusion John Wolfe wrote for his how-to article about speaking in public, which ran in *Reader's Digest:*

The old saying, "practice makes perfect," applies in public speaking too.

So speak at every opportunity; the rewards can be enormous. Indeed, with practice, you can use speaking as a springboard to success and a fuller, more satisfying life.

Author Jennie Renfrow wrote a first-person piece in *G., The Magazine of Gainesville* detailing the pleasures and problems of living together before marriage. Here's her summary conclusion.

At this point in our lives, it has provided us with what we need: love, security, stability and friendship. It has taught us to communicate, share and be flexible with each other.

We know whether or not we *do* get married in the future, we'll have had this time together. In this uncertain world, that's something to value.

Poetic

In this type of conclusion, the writer tries for something symbolic or otherwise thought-provoking, a quote or anecdote or grand statement that delivers the ultimate (or at least final) insight or sobering thought. The following example is from Aura Bland's article on the hoboes of Gainesville, Florida, and how they're treated there.

In front of St. Francis Hall, Joe McDole was eating his free peanut butter sandwich. A student walked by and yelled, "Why don't you bums get a job?"

"Why don't you get me a job or shut your mouth!" McDole yelled back.

The student laughed and walked on by.

"He laughs because he doesn't understand," McDole said. "He is afraid of what he doesn't understand, so he laughs to cover up his fear. He should be afraid, because anyone can snap and feel they can't cope anymore if they experience enough pain and disappointment.

"Anybody can turn to the streets," McDole said.

To end his story on missing children and the emotional wreckage they leave behind, Associated Press writer Tad Bartimus used this insightful conclusion, quoting the mother of one of the vanished teen-agers.

"You think nothing like this could ever happen to you," she said. "When it does, at first you can't believe it. But slowly you just sink into this depression, where you exist one day at a time, hoping that tomorrow, at last, you'll know what happened to your child."

Writer Theresa Waldron, in a piece about the controversy over Georgia-Pacific Corporation's proposal to mine peat from a north Florida swamp, first presented the Georgia-Pacific representative, then those who would be affected by the proposed peat mining. Here's her poetic, symbolic conclusion to the piece, which ran in the *Journal of Soil and Water Conservation*. (The complete article is reprinted on pp. 118–122.)

Darkness settled around us as we reached Hill's modest home, which sits ranch-style amid red and yellow flowers dotting a well-manicured lawn.

Fireflies darted near redwood chairs placed haphazardly at the water's edge. His grandchildren had put them there, Hill said.

We shook hands, and I made my way toward the driveway, where my car was parked. I thought of Hill's battle to save a small patch of a large planet, and how he believes in the interdependence of water, soil, and air. I thought about how he wanted his grandchildren to fish the swamp streams as he once did.

I turned and waved to Hill, who was standing on his front porch. He waved back, then flipped a switch, lighting my way.

Futuristic

This type concludes by turning the reader's attention toward the future, hopefully, challengingly, or by simply saying, in effect, that the beat goes on. The following example is from a feature by *Florida Times-Union* writer Sharon R. McGriff about a young mother in Jacksonville who killed her baby and herself in an act of desperate loneliness.

The lead.

When the maintenance foreman unlocked the apartment door on Jan. 26, Kathy Tribune's Bible lay open to Psalms 69:3—"I am weary of my crying; my throat is dried; mine eyes fail while I wait for my God."

A few feet away, under the coffee table in the living room, lay the bodies of Ms. Tribune and her 11-month-old daughter, Christine Shalamurra.

Dr. Peter Lipkovic of the Medical Examiner's Office ruled last week that the 31-year-old mother had stabbed her baby several times with a kitchen knife and then turned the knife on herself. She slowly bled to death from superficial chest wounds.

The conclusion quotes the executive director of a charitable agency.

Johnson, however, said the deaths left him with a question: "What becomes of the Kathies of the world? Most of us are so unconcerned; business goes on as usual. But until we change our attitudes, there will be a lot of Kathies."

To end her article on Pierce Brodkorb, an expert on prehistoric birds and collector of their fossilized remains, writer Susan Kay Jacobson used this quote from Brodkorb as a futuristic, the-beat-goes-on conclusion:

"... I have so many bones still left to look at. I'll never finish. So much remains to be discovered about the evolution of birds."

That's That

This type of conclusion is commonly used in continuous narrative and other pieces organized chronologically. It has the effect of bringing the day, the adventure, the case—or whatever—to a close, as well as ending the piece. Here's one such conclusion written by Norbert Slepyan in his first-person article on flying an ultralight airplane. The piece ran in *GEO* magazine.

Power all back, the wheels touch, touch again and are planted. I cut the switch, and the Vector stops. I am on the grass strip. I have just landed *across* a runway and stopped while still on it. Outstanding! The roll-out hasn't been anticlimactic. It hasn't been at all.

In the brisk breeze, I unhook my helmet, undo my straps, disconnect my radio and wait in my bucket. I am whole, home and happy.

Writer Terrie Riecke used a that's-that conclusion in her article about Fred Strong, the Florida garbage man. The piece was built around an interview and organized chronologically. Here's the conclusion:

Then Strong gave his last wide-grinned, teeth-flashing, throaty laugh as his brown boots crunched their way across the sand and gravel to a long-awaited weekend. No more garbage days until Monday.

See What I Mean?

This type of conclusion presents the author's final pitch to the reader, one last illustration to make the point of the piece. Here's an example, from an article lawyer-writer John Sansing did for *The Washingtonian*. The piece was a collection of anecdotes showing the zaniness that occurs in the District of Columbia courthouse. One of the colorful courthouse characters singled out was a defense lawyer named Ken Robinson. After a few more anecdotes, author Sansing brought himself into the piece and offered the following concluding anecdote on the comical aspects of criminal justice:

I only occasionally go back, to accept a case or two each year. When I do return for a case, I fancy myself much more experienced and capable that when I showed up ten years ago, with tons of theory and not one ounce of street smarts, and was handed my first criminal case: a sodomy charge against a man named – I swear – Buggs. Now I know my craft.

Take the case I handled last year. A judge asked me to defend a participant in a grudge killing. The killing had taken place the previous year, and in the meantime my client had been convicted of another crime and sent out of the jurisdiction. It took several weeks to transfer him back to Washington, and I began to prepare the case in his absence.

I hired an investigator, who soon produced eyewitness interview affidavits. I obtained full discovery from the prosecutor. I recognized the strengths and weaknesses of our case and prepared a series of motions designed to suppress statements and evidence I felt had been illegally obtained. By the time my client arrived, my work was nearly finished.

The morning of this first hearing, I rushed down to the basement cellblock and introduced myself.

"Joe," I began, "my name is Sansing—here's my card. You're charged with first-degree murder, a man named Avon Little. It's an old case, so here's the motion to dismiss for lack of speedy trial I'm filing. The statement you gave was not voluntary, so here's the motion to suppress it I'm filing. I need three witnesses—here are their names—and I want you to help me find their addresses and telephone numbers. I've got statements from the other witnesses, so we're in good shape there. We go upstairs in a few minutes and I'll plead not-guilty for you. No use arguing the bond question, since you've got two years left on that other charge anyway. We'll be back in court in three weeks for a status hearing, and trial is set for June 15. Anything I can do for you?"

My new client silently listened to my speech and looked at my card and at the motions and lists of witnesses I had presented to him. Finally he spoke.

"One thing I'd like you to do for me. Take down the telephone number of my father."

I wrote it down.

"Go upstairs, call him, and give him this message."

I waited expectantly.

"Get Ken Robinson."

Here's the see-what-I-mean conclusion an anonymous Associated Press writer put on his feature about Ray Bedal, who at five feet is the shortest police officer in Dade County, Florida. The piece detailed some of his experiences as a short cop, then ended with this quote from him:

"My only problem is getting in my mailbox. They gave me the one on top. It's been that way all my life."

In a *Reader's Digest* article countering claims that Yuri Andropov, the former top man in the Kremlin, was not really such a bad guy, John Barron built a documented case for believing Andropov to be a ruthless, merciless, humorless, and dangerous foe of democracy. The author ended his piece with this see-what-I-mean conclusion:

While waiting to see what Andropov will do, we should remember that his smile and courteous words do not always mean what they seem. When he served as ambassador in Hungary, the Budapest police department had a gypsy band and Andropov sometimes called Police Chief Sandor Kopacsi to ask that it play at the Soviet embassy. On November 5, 1956, Chief Kopacsi and his wife were captured as they fled toward refuge in the Yugoslav embassy. They were taken to Andropov. "He met us rather cordially," Kopacsi recalls. But then, as the KGB hauled him off to prison, Kopacsi looked back and saw Andropov standing at the embassy gate, smiling and waving to him. Kopacsi spent the next seven years behind bars.

See what I mean?

Writing in First Person

A SIMPLE RULE GUIDES the writer trying to decide whether to write the piece using first person: Make sure there's a good reason. If the piece can be written as easily and effectively without resort to first person, don't use it.

Journalism especially and nonfiction generally are meant to serve the reader, not the writer's ego or other self-interest. The writer's role is that of storyteller, and that usually should be satisfying enough. Putting oneself into a feature or article is not something to be done to call attention to or glamorize the writer. Neither is it to be done without carefully considering angle and organization—without considering, in other words, the best way to tell the story.

Although first person comes in a variety of forms, some are more journalistically justifiable than others. Here are the most common ones.

Types of First Person Writing

GONZO. In this variety, the writer does not necessarily write about the subject; instead, he writes about himself covering the subject or otherwise in relation to the subject. The resulting piece may have little coverage, or even mention, of the purported subject. Instead, the author self-consciously turns the spotlight on himself.

Gonzo first person should be considered only when the writer is more interesting or more important than the subject. Gonzo is exemplified by much of the work of writer Hunter S. Thompson, especially including his article which later became the book *Fear and Loathing in Las Vegas.* An excerpt from an article Thompson did for *Scanlan's Monthly* on the Kentucky Derby illustrates the type:

With 30 hours to post time I had no press credentials and—according to the sports editor of the Louisville Courier-Journal—no hope at all of getting any.

Worse, I needed two sets; one for myself and another for Ralph Steadman, the English illustrator who was coming from London to do some Derby drawings. All I knew about him was that this was his first visit to the United States. And the more I pondered that fact, the more it gave me fear. Would he bear up under the heinous culture shock of being lifted out of London and plunged into a drunken mob scene at the Kentucky Derby? There was no way of knowing. Hopefully, he would arrive at least a day or so ahead, and give himself time to get acclimated. Maybe a few hours of peaceful sightseeing in the Bluegrass country around Lexington. My plan was to pick him up at the airport in the huge Pontiac Ballbuster I'd rented from a used car salesman named Colonel Quick, then whisk him off to some peaceful setting to remind him of England.

Colonel Quick had solved the car problem, and money (four times the normal rate) had bought two rooms in a scumbox on the outskirts of town. The only other kink was the task of convincing the moguls at Churchill Downs that *Scanlan's* was such a prestigious sporting journal that common sense compelled them to give us two sets of the best press tickets. This was not easily done. My first call to the publicity office resulted in total failure. The press handler was shocked at the idea that anyone would be stupid enough to apply for press credentials two days before the Derby. "Hell, you can't be serious," he said. "The deadline was two months ago. The press box is full; there's no more room . . . and what the hell is *Scanlan's Monthly* anyway?"

I uttered a painful groan. "Didn't the London office call you? They're flying an artist over to do the paintings. Steadman. He's Irish, I think. Very famous over there. I just got in from the Coast. The San Francisco office told me we were all set."

He seemed interested, and even sympathetic, but there was nothing he could do. I flattered him with more gibberish, and finally he offered a compromise: he could get us two passes to the clubhouse grounds.

"That sounds a little weird," I said. "It's unacceptable. We *must* have access to everything. *All* of it. The spectacle, the people, the pageantry and certainly the race. You don't think we came all this way to watch the damn thing on television, do you? One way or another we'll get inside . . .

HE (SHE) WAS TALKING TO ME. In this kind of first-person usage, the writer explains that the source addressed his words to the writer, as in this example:

> Consuela, now 20 and a nursing student at the University of South Florida, had grown up with the nickname of "Moose." "It's kind of hard to always be the biggest kid in your class," she told me.
>
> I asked her if she was conscious of being overweight. "I usually didn't think about my size too much," she answered.

Ordinarily there's no justification for the writer to intrude in such a way. The reader will assume the source was speaking to the interviewer, and it's not necessary—and usually not fitting—for the writer to enter the story in such cases.

INTEGRAL CHARACTER. Sometimes, to set up an anecdote or dialogue that shows something about the subject, the writer may use first person to cast himself as a minor but (for the purposes of the article) necessary character in the scene recreated in the piece. Here's an example from a Q&A piece by writer MaryAnne·Golon:

Alachua County Sheriff Lu Hindery surprised me when he answered the phone. Instead of the usual screening by a secretary, the sheriff himself was on the line.

I told him I wanted to talk to him about crime in Alachua County in an interview.

"Well, I guess that would be all right," he said. "How about next Wednesday at eleven?"

"That's fine," I said. "I'm going to need about an hour."

"An hour!" he exclaimed, and I was suddenly afraid of my chances of getting it. "I'm a busy man, you know!" he said gruffly – then let out a laugh, as if mocking his own importance. "Guess we better make it about ten-thirty then. Okay?"

Okay, I thought – both for the time and for the sheriff.

PERSONAL EXPERIENCE. This one is the major kind of first-person writing. It is usually a story of some sort of adventure in which the writer is *the* major character or *a* major character. The writer has become both reporter and source, as in this excerpt from writer Julie Petzold's feature on spelunking.

By the time Saturday, the day of our adventure, arrived, I had had three days to conjure up every possible thought of what could happen to me in a cave. When my alarm went off at 9 a.m., I awoke with the scary reality that today I was going to explore Warren's Cave, the longest dry cave in Florida, with three miles of dry shallow tunnels extending 110 feet below the surface.

Now, as I dressed in old jeans and sneakers, worries of all kinds sped through my head. Would I survive the trip? Would my eyes and hair be pecked away by bats? How long would it take a rescue squad to find us? Those thoughts were still running through my head as I left my apartment to meet with my fellow spelunkers while my less adventuresome friends hollered good luck and promised to attend my funeral. It was no time to kid.

Our rendezvous point was in northwest Gainesville, deep in a forest. There were eight of us; I was the only girl.

GHOST STORY. This kind of first-person usage also relates a personal experience, but the writer is merely reporter and writer, not the person who had the experience. Here the writer enters a partnership: he contributes his storytelling ability, and his source contributes his personal experience. The resulting piece is written under the byline of the person who had the experience.

The following example is the story of a lawyer named Hamilton H. Whaley, published in *Guideposts* magazine, which specializes in first-person, personal-experience stories. The actual author of the piece gathered the facts from Whaley in an interview, then wrote the article under Whaley's byline.

I T MIGHT seem strange that although I am a healthy 56 years old, and an experienced lawyer, I'm living today in an orphanage in Savannah, Georgia. But it's true, and all because one day I read my own obituary.

In September 1976, I was happily married, had five great kids (all but one of them grown), had a big, comfortable house in a pleasant community where we had lived for 25 years, was a member of a fine church, and was making more money than I'd ever dreamed of. I held a job that seemed to me the pinnacle of my profession—a partner in one of the leading law firms in Tampa, Florida, a vast organization with nearly 70 lawyers.

It was a secure and satisfying position I'd arrived at, made all the more so by the fact that I'd come the long, hard way to get there. I was an orphan. I had grown up in an orphanage, where I'd been placed when I was six years old. But I was pleased with the way things had worked out for me.

Then came that day in September, and the whole course of my life was changed.

I was on my way to an appointment, driving along a main road, when suddenly an elderly man in a big car pulled out from a dirt lane, right in front of me. My little Subaru crashed into the side of his car, and I was knocked unconscious.

After a short stay in the hospital, I went home, conscious but wobbly and a little fuzzy in the head. Ten days after the accident, while I was still recovering at home, the telephone rang, and my wife Betty answered it.

"Mrs. Whaley," the caller said, "this is Judge Tidwell. I just read in the Hillsborough County Bar Association *Bulletin* about your husband's death. I want to express my regrets."

Betty was taken aback at first, then told him there must have been some

mistake, that I was all right, though still not able to resume my work.

Pretty soon the phone rang again. Someone else was calling to offer condolences. Then we began getting one call after another, and I started looking for my copy of the bar association paper, to see what this was all about.

I found it and, sure enough, there on the first page, under a bold, black headline—In Memoriam—was my death notice: "Hamilton H. Whaley." Obviously, there had been some mixup, but I felt as if I were reading my own tombstone. It was like an advance notice of my death. I fought off a wave of squeamishness by trying to joke about it.

"Now I know how Mark Twain felt when he said reports of his death were greatly exaggerated," I said, smiling.

Actually, I felt suddenly sobered, realizing just how close I had come to getting killed. Fortunately, I'd been driving at the speed limit, something I didn't always do. Having been an insurance lawyer for a long time, I knew what another 10 miles an hour would have done to that little car of mine—and, in that case, the death notice would have been terribly accurate. It was disturbing to think how quickly life could be ended.

That thought stayed with me for weeks. I found myself imagining the world without Hamilton Whaley in it, and I began to be bothered by the question, if I were suddenly to die, would there be anything left behind to show that my life had made a difference?

One day I was taking a deposition from a man who had been injured on the job, a bricklayer about my age. I was going down the form, asking the standard questions:

"What is your name?"

"Your address?"

"What is your occupation?"

It was necessary also to know how

long he had been doing that sort of work and the specifics of the job.

"Give me your work history," I said to him, and explained the kind of information I needed.

He told me he'd been a brickmason for 30 years, that he'd worked on some of the biggest buildings in town, that he'd spent five years putting up the brick on one building complex. He reeled off a list of buildings he'd worked on, many of which were familiar to me.

My gosh, I thought, feeling envious, *this man's literally got monumemts he'll leave behind when he goes. What have I got?*

All I had, I felt, were file drawers full of folders representing hundreds of industrial insurance cases, each of which would be thrown away two years after the case was closed. *A life ought to count for more than file folders,* I thought.

Of course, there were my children, and I was proud of them. There were also the boys I taught in Sunday school, six-year-olds. I loved those kids and I knew that working with them was important.

Even so, I grew more and more restless. I started praying about it. "Lord," I said, "what am I supposed to be doing? Help me to know."

In October 1979, our church in Tampa put on a missions conference, and a missionary was the main speaker. I sat there listening to him say things that put into words the undefined tugs I was feeling inside. The message to me was clear: God wanted more service from me, something more than my everyday routine.

I got up from the pew and walked to the altar, knelt, and told the Lord my life was His, that I was turning it over to Him to use as He saw fit. "I'll do whatever You have for me," I said.

When we got home that night, I told Betty what I'd done. "I want to serve the Lord," I said. "But what in the world can a 53-year-old lawyer do for Him?"

Betty didn't have the answer either.

"The only thing I know to do is keep praying about it," she said. And that we did.

I also studied my Bible, searching for a clue. There were several Scripture passages that I kept going back to. One was Galatians 6:7, "Be not deceived; God is not mocked: for whatsoever a man soweth, that shall he also reap." The more I thought about it the more I knew that I didn't want to just sow files.

That image of "planting" stuck with me. I thought of how I had been cared for at the orphanage in South Carolina. Maybe there was some way I could "plant" myself back into an orphans' home, to take what it had produced—me—and give it back to help some needy kids of the present generation.

One Sunday while visiting Betty's sister in Toccoa, Georgia, we attended a Christian and Missionary Alliance church. During the evening service, the pastor announced to the congregation that there was a young man there who had a message he'd like to deliver, and he called him up to the platform.

The young man's name was Mike Moore, and he had been a student at Toccoa Falls College. After he'd graduated, he had taken a job at a boys' home in Savannah. With a week off, he had come back to see friends in Toccoa, visit his old home church and, while there, make a simple announcement that Bethesda Home for Boys, where he worked, a private, Christian institution that dates back to 1740, was looking for good people to serve as houseparents.

"It doesn't make any difference how old you are or how young you are," he said, "if you really are called for this kind of work."

Betty and I looked at each other, dumbfounded. Here we were, 650 miles from home, on a search for just such a position, and on the one Sunday that we happened to be in this church, this man also happened to be there saying, in effect, "We're looking for you."

It was the most remarkable answer to prayer I'd ever heard of.

Betty and I went to Savannah and visited the Bethesda Home for Boys. We met with the director and assistant director, and learned something of the history of the place and how it operated. There are seven "cottages," more like large residences than cottages, with up to 20 boys from 5 to 18 years of age and a pair of houseparents living in each.

It was up to the houseparents to exert a Christian influence on the boys, to set an example, take them to church, lead them in family devotions, help them with their problems. Except for cooking meals—everyone ate at the central dining hall—the job was pretty much like being parents of a huge family of boys.

On December 31, 1980, I resigned officially from my law firm in Tampa. Betty and I disposed of our house, gave up our responsibilities at church, ended our commitments in the community, did a lot of explaining to our friends, and moved, along with our teenage son

David, to Bethesda. On January 1, 1981, we became houseparents to the 16 boys of Alumni Cottage, a rambling brick residence that sits among the huge oaks.

We have loved it from the moment we arrived here. We feel we are a blessing to the boys, and they are a blessing to us. We are erecting buildings of living stones. If we're successful with any of these boys, then his life and, someday, his wife's life and his children's lives will all be affected, perhaps for generations to come.

I try to give the boys in our cottage a feeling of worth, a feeling that they're loved, that God cares about them very much, and that I do too.

This, I believe, is the Lord's work, and He called me to do it.

I believe that for nearly 50 years He guided me toward this place, from the time I was a frightened six-year-old orphan. Now I'm where God wants me, in a life that began—instead of ending—with my obituary.

STRUCTURAL. In this usage, the writer enters the story to organize the piece, becoming a link between segments of the story and a source for some of the material.

In the following example, published in the *Journal of Soil and Water Conservation,* Theresa Waldron faced the question of how to effectively bring together in one article both sides of a controversy that involved a proposal by the Georgia-Pacific Corporation to mine peat from a north Florida swamp. She decided to write the piece in first person, letting herself link the two opposite viewpoints.

THERE was a crisp chill in the October air as we stepped from the Ford Bronco onto the mushy trail leading into the Santa Fe Swamp in Bradford County, Florida. As I gazed into the dense pine and palmetto forest, which didn't look like a swamp at all, the CB radio inside the vehicle blared, "Paul, can you read me?"

Paul White, 52, the land acquisitions manager and geologist for Georgia-Pacific Corporation's Palatka pulp mill, interrupted his preparations for

our journey into the swamp and leaned into the Bronco toward the radio.

"Ten-four, I read you," White announced into the CB's microphone.

"What were those ratios on pine and hardwood for last month again?" the voice on the radio asked.

"The pine was up, and the hardwood was about the same as the month before," White responded. He turned to me and said he didn't remember the exact figures.

"They tell me we're up about 13 million on the pine," the voice told White.

"Sounds about right to me," White replied.

"Y'all don't get lost out there," the radio voice said.

"We won't. Ten-four," White said.

White moved again to the rear of the truck and pulled a two-foot-long machete out of the Bronco. He slammed the door shut, turned to me and said. "Ready?"

"Ready," I answered.

I followed this tall, athletic, white-haired man along the narrow, roughly hewn trail into a 5,000-acre tract of densely wooded land, into a swamp I was not even vaguely familiar with. I was there because I wanted to see the land that Georgia-Pacific had purchased two years earlier with the intention of mining it for peat to burn as fuel at its mill in nearby Palatka.

"Watch your step," White warned. "Here comes the wet part."

Wet it was. We were less than 50 yards from the truck, and already we were ankle deep in soft, brown, foul-smelling muck. My sneakers immediately filled with water, and my feet sucked in and out of the muck with each step. We were wading through water and peat on a narrow trail that White had helped clear a year earlier. I followed him blindly as he hacked at limbs and thorny branches and told me where to step.

"If you sink down, don't panic," he said. "I'll help you out. If you can swim, you're all right."

Within 20 minutes, we were knee deep, and our progress slowed. I noticed that the water was greener with slimy moss and that we often came across little hills of roots. They were difficult to climb over because my jeans were heavy and waterlogged, making each step an effort.

"Those are tussocks," White said of the small root hills. "I usually end up tripping over their roots."

Long strands of whip-like bushes surrounded the trail: I hung onto them for balance. Twice I sank into the muck

to my hips; White gave me his hand and pulled me out.

"Is this quicksand?" I anxiously asked. The only swamp I had ever seen was in the old Tarzan movies, and quicksand then meant almost certain death.

"No, not really. I've known people to sink in up to their necks, though," he said.

White picked up a handful of the muck and squeezed it; the brown water flowed out from between his fingers.

"Peat absorbs 40 percent of its own weight in water," he said. "But when it's dried, it won't reabsorb water."

White said his corporation wants to clear the swamp, drain all the surface water out through ditches and canals, and harvest the peat a half-inch at a time. Combine-like implements will suck up the dry, dusty peat and form it into bricks, which will then be burned in boilers at the Palatka mill, much as coal is.

"With rising fuel costs, we wanted a good alternative energy source," White said. "In Finland, they've been harvesting peat for years, and we've used their methods as a model."

As a hawk circled overhead, I asked White about the effects of peat harvesting on the swamp's wildlife.

"There is no wildlife in the swamp. A fish and wildlife game officer came out and told us that. There is game on the quarter-mile perimeter of the swamp, and we will preserve that area for them," he said.

I asked how far we'd come, and he told me a half a mile. The swamp is three and a half miles across. I told him I was ready to turn back. My legs seemed to weigh 100 pounds each, and my feet were numb with cold.

"I come out here every chance I get," he told me. "I'm a real nature boy at heart."

White, who earned a bachelor's degree in geology and forestry at the University of Florida in 1958, led me back to the truck. The return trip seemed twice as long, though I did not sink into the muck any deeper than my knees.

When we reached the truck, about two hours after starting our journey, White had a thermos of hot coffee waiting. The thermos had a printed message on it, "Working together . . . Georgia-Pacific Corporation."

As I pulled off my socks and sneakers, cupfuls of brown water flowed onto the ground. We sipped coffee.

I asked White what he thought of the environmentalists' opposition to the mining proposal.

"I'm an environmentalist myself. I wouldn't be here if I thought the corporation was going against the environment," he commented.

He told me a story about a friend's ancestor, a farmer who introduced kudzu into Alabama as cattle feed.

"If I thought I was like that fella who gave future generations kudzu with this mining proposal, I wouldn't be able to face my grandchildren. We're following environmental guidelines with this thing, and it won't affect the future in a bad way. If it weren't environmentally sound, Georgia-Pacific wouldn't harvest the peat. We invite constructive criticism, and we are now taking safeguards for the future with agency review and, hopefully, approval," White explained.

He said the corporation was compiling a preliminary study at a peat area called Cow Bay in Putnam County, which would need the approval of 32 environmental agencies before the Santa Fe Swamp could be mined. The agencies would also have to approve the swamp proposal, he said, under regulations concerning wildlife management, water drainage, and effect on nearby waterways.

"We have applied for permits from two regulatory agencies for the Cow Bay project," he said, "and we will go along with their recommendations."

White reminded me that Georgia-Pacific had won several awards for its safe harvesting of trees in the Southeast and for giving parcels of land to the state for park use.

White then drove me back to my car. When I got behind the wheel, I quickly turned on the heater full force. My feet didn't thaw out until I reached home in Gainesville, 30 miles away.

IT was late one August afternoon when Harold Hill steered us in his motorboat to the perimeter of the Santa Fe Swamp on the north side of Santa Fe Lake.

"Look at the osprey," he said. "That's a fish eagle. He makes his home in the swamp. There's his nest."

Hill pointed to a tall cypress, where in its highest branches a large, gray bird perched on the edge of a nest.

Hill, 58, a slender, energetic, gray-haired man, is the president of the Santa Fe Lake Dwellers Association, a group of several hundred lakefront property owners who unanimously oppose the swamp mining proposal. Hill circulated a petition last year against the project, with all but one lake dweller's signature on it.

"The only one who wouldn't sign the petition was a Georgia-Pacific employee," Hill said. "We have more than 5,000 signatures from concerned area citizens on the petition too."

Hill turned off the boat's motor, and we drifted to the sounds of crickets and water lapping the edges of the boat. I pointed to a stream that appeared to lead into the swamp from the lake.

"Oh, yes, that's a stream all right," he said. "I fished it as a boy. It goes right into the swamp, and anybody who says there's no fish in there doesn't know what they're talking about."

Hill reached over and started the motor once again.

"Let me show you something," he said.

He guided us over to a small, sandy beach, one of hundreds bordering the lake.

"That man got into trouble when he put that sand in there," he said. "The U.S. Army Corps of Engineers said he disturbed the wild grasses and the drainage there, and he had to fix it. They're very strict with us."

A retired branch manager for the Jacksonville Water Service Division, Hill has lived on the lake for 17 years and near the lake all of his life. He said the Corps of Engineers was just one agency that would rule in his organization's favor against the proposed mining.

"If they won't let that homeowner tear up a small patch of grass on his own property, how will they allow 5,000 acres to be ruined?" he asked.

We were in the center of the lake, and Hill slowed the boat to an idle. He turned on a small depth gauge on the dashboard of the boat. It registered 18 feet.

"If they drain the swamp, there will be runoff and subsequent flooding all the way to the Gulf. But we will be the worst ones affected."

The swamp acts like a sponge, Hill explained. Once the water is drained, the lake will dry out because the peat helps to maintain the water level of the lake by feeding the lake and surrounding waterways.

"The contaminants and heavy metals that the peat normally filters will get into the groundwater and rivers and will jeopardize our rivers and lakes as we now know them," he added.

With the motor off again, we drifted on the lake. The breeze brought sounds of children playing near the water's edge, some distance away. Hill leaned forward in his seat and rested his arms on his knees, facing the swamp.

"My nephew belongs to a hunting club that hunts near the swamp. He's seen panthers and bears there, and there have been documented bald eagle sightings right in the swamp itself," he said.

Hill has been traveling the state since the petition started, "telling anyone who will listen that we won't stand for this mining."

He told me that in his travels across the northern and central parts of Florida he had spoken to city and county commissions and obtained 11 resolutions against the proposal from them. He also said he had Governor Bob Graham's word that the governor would not let the proposal pass if it came to legislative approval and that seven state senators and representatives also opposed mining.

"We have submitted a proposal to the governor asking that Georgia-Pacific be the willing seller of the swamp to the state, which has right of eminent domain over the land," Hill said.

It began to get dark as we headed back to Hill's dock. The sky behind us turned pink, and the breeze appeared cooler against my face. I asked Hill the main reason he opposes the mining proposal.

"It took 10,000 years to make that swamp, and it will take only a few years to destroy it. As a new source of energy for the Palatka mill, at best the peat will only last until the next century. It's not a good trade-off for the havoc it will create on the soil, water, and air quality here. I believe in clean water and air, and a place for wildlife to live, and we can have it if we can consider methods of control. But most of all, I want my grandchildren to know a clean environment," he said.

Before the boat trip, Hill had shown me reams of research from environmental groups that had studied the effects of peat mining in this country and in Europe.

"We have the Sierra Club, the National Wetlands Technical Council, and the National Wildlife Federation on our side, to name a few," he said.

As we reached the dock, Hill hopped out of the boat and quickly moored it to a wooden piling. He asked if I needed help getting out of the boat, but I declined, easily making the two-foot jump to the dock.

Darkness settled around us as we reached Hill's modest home, which sits ranch-style amid red and yellow flowers dotting a well-manicured lawn. Fireflies darted near redwood chairs placed haphazardly at the water's edge. His grandchildren had put them there, Hill said.

We shook hands, and I made my way toward the driveway, where my car was parked. I thought of Hill's battle to save a small patch of a large planet, and how he believes in the interdependence of water, soil, and air. I thought about how he wanted his grandchildren to fish the swamp streams as he once did.

I turned and waved to Hill, who was standing on his front porch. He waved back, then flipped a switch, lighting my way.

Advantages and Disadvantages of First-Person Writing

Gonzo is for such a special kind of first-person piece that it need not be considered by a writer trying to decide how to best tell the story. He-said-it-to-me usage of first person is, in most cases, an abuse, and there's no good reason for using it. Integral-character usage generally does not affect the piece significantly in form or substance and in many cases is unavoidable – unless scenes involving the writer are simply left out.

The three other varieties of first person, however, often present actual alternatives to the ordinary third-person feature or article. If the story might be best told by one of those, the writer should certainly consider doing so.

There are at least four major advantages of first person.

1. It provides an eyewitness account. For authenticity and authoritativeness, it's hard to beat a story that says, in effect, "I was there. I saw it. I heard it." An account filled with hard detail is far more believable. In the personal-experience and structural usages of first person, the writer is able to become his own primary source and can deliver the eyewitness material undiluted and unfiltered, straight to the reader.

2. It creates a sense of intimacy. By using first person, the writer in effect takes the reader into his confidence, revealing details from his experience. The sense of intimacy that results ordinarily makes it easier for the reader to identify with the story's major character and enter into the story's situation.

3. It allows subjectivity. Since the writer is telling the story from his perspective in first person, his interpretations, impressions, and feelings are permissable. In a piece written in third person, however, such material from the author could be considered unacceptable editorialization and out of place. For example, in MaryAnne Golon's article on Sheriff Lu Hindery (excerpted in the integral-character illustration) the writer, by using first person, was able to tell the reader how it seemed to her.

> "An hour!" he exclaimed, and I was suddenly afraid of my chances of getting it. "I'm a busy man, you know!" he

said gruffly—then let out a laugh, as if
mocking his own importance. "Guess
we better make it about ten-thirty
then. Okay?"
Okay, I thought—both for the time
and for the sheriff.

First person allowed the writer to convey her impression of the sheriff,
helping the reader see him in the same way.

4. It provides structure. Writing in first person ordinarily means telling about someone's experiences—the writer's or someone else's. Stories
of experiences can be told chronologically. If not organized chronologically, the piece may be structured thematically, presenting the writer's
experiences arranged by category: best, next best, next best after that,
for example; or pro then con. Theresa Waldron's article on the peat-
mining controversy is an example of a first-person piece providing structure by presenting the pro material, then the con. The author acts as a
bridge between the two.

First person has its faults, however. Its two major disadvantages:

1. It offers a limited view. Since the story is told from one person's
perspective, the writer can ordinarily show only what *he* saw, tell only
what *he* heard, or describe only what *he* felt. For example, if the writer—
or the person to whom the first-person "I" refers—was asleep or unconscious or in another room or another city while some important part of the
action was occurring, it's difficult to present that necessary material to
the reader. The reader will be following the "I" and can only be where the
"I" is. In the examples above, the "I" and the reader are out of it. Events
unknown to the "I" ordinarily cannot be known to the reader.

Of course, there are devices for solving the problem. The "I" could
say something like, "I didn't know it at the time, but in Peoria the effects
were already being felt," then reveal the then-unknown material. The "I"
eventually gets the information, but for storytelling purposes, it must
come in chronological sequence so the reader gets it in the same order as
it unfolded in reality. First person frequently runs into such limited-view
problems, and each time it does, the writer must devise a solution.

2. It lacks journalistic detachment. Some of the advantage gained by
allowing subjectivity in a first-person piece may be offset by its obvious
loss of objectivity, usually an estimable goal of American journalism.
Third-person narrative permits the writer a dispassionate, clear-headed
detachment from the events and characters of the story. The third-person
narrator is only a storyteller to the reader. The first-person narrator, on
the other hand, is involved in the story, and the continual use of first-
person pronouns can have the subtle effect of reducing grand historical
fact to merely one person's story. A reader might suspect it is for just that

reason some writers – Norman Mailer in his book, *Armies of the Night,* for example – choose to write about themselves in third person when they have been involved in the story's action and scenes.

A writer should think of first person as one more tool to help him do the best possible job. In cases where it is exactly what is needed to tell a story, the writer can choose it knowing fully what it will do.

Brite Writing

TULSA, Okla. – For a moment, Lucille Ainsle felt buffaloed when she opened the door of her Tulsa home.

Thursday morning while she was still in bed, she heard a strange commotion outside. She got up, went to the door and, opening it, found herself staring into the face of a half-ton heifer buffalo, which had escaped from a nearby ranch.

After the buffalo was retrieved by its owner, who is planning to raise buffalo, Ainsle recognized her plight. "I didn't know what it was at first," she said. "I thought it was a big cow with hair on its face."

THAT'S A BRITE. Brites are the smallest variety of feature story, built around one quickly told incident that has in it something quirky. The incident has a clear element of irony, humor, or great oddity – or a combination of those.

A brite is the writer's way of looking at an item of news. For example, a reporter, having learned the facts about the escaped buffalo, could have written a straight news story, with an ordinary news lead and the additional factual information arranged in inverted-pyramid fashion beneath the lead – a no-kidding-around handling of the event. Instead, the writer saw the oddity in the incident, then wrote the story so the reader could see it too.

What Brites Are Good For

Brites serve several purposes in newspapers and are generally prized by the editors who are responsible for putting the issue together. For one thing – their main reason for being – they provide comic relief to ordinary news, which has a natural tendency to be heavy. Brites have a way of piercing black clouds to cast tiny rays of sunshine across the page.

They also have a couple of mechanical functions. A brite can be set in a ruled box and placed on the newspaper page to separate or stagger headlines of similar styles in adjoining columns. Placing similar headlines side by side in adjoining columns is called tombstoning, or bumping, headlines and is generally believed by editors to be an esthetic breach. Brites help avoid the breach.

Brites also make excellent fillers. When a bigger story is not long enough to reach to the bottom of the column, an editor can plunk a brite into the remaining space, solving a makeup problem for himself and giving the reader a treat at the same time.

How Brites Are Put Together

Well done brites follow a simple, unvarying three-part outline:
1. Lead.
2. Anecdote relating the incident.
3. Conclusion.
Here's how a brite about a police car follows that outline:
The lead.

> Police are not only protectors of our community, but can also be disturbers of our peace.

The anecdote relating the incident.

The Gustafson family of 616 College Hill Dr., Clearwater, was celebrating their Fourth of July dinner with three guests when they heard a loud crash outside.

Thinking someone had run into their car in the driveway, Nanci Gustafson, their 21-year-old daughter, ran outside to inspect the damage. When she got outside and didn't see any damage to the car, she walked around to the side of the house and found a police car rammed into the house, a demolished cement block planter at the corner of the house and a damaged living room wall.

The policeman, unhurt, explained that the car had slipped into drive after he had screeched to a halt while pursuing an armed suspect in a drug bust. The patrol car had then proceeded driverless up hill into the side of the house.

The Conclusion.

"I always thought police were supposed to stop disturbances," Nanci said, "not cause them."

Here's another brite, from United Press International, which will serve as a contrast to the police car brite:

C O P E N H A G E N – (U P I) –For little Tobias Gravergaard it must have been a rude awakening.

The seven-year-old boy was fast asleep in the back of his mother's car as it sped along a highway near Copenhagen when suddenly the door swung open and Tobias tumbled out.

The door shut behind him and the car continued on its way without Eva Gravergaard's even noticing that Tobias was missing.

About 15 minutes and 12 miles later she looked in the back seat for her sleeping son.

No Tobias.

She swung the car around and rushed back in search of the boy.

When she found him, Tobias was sitting quietly on the side of the road, being looked after by the drivers of two cars that were behind his when he made his exit. Tobias suffered only a broken leg from the accident.

One of the first things to be noticed about the little Tobias brite is that, like the police car incident, it could have been handled as a straight news story. The writer, however, saw the incident as an oddity and wrote it as a brite.

Something else to be noticed: There's no conclusion. The brite has a Part 1, the lead; and a Part 2, the anecdote relating the incident. Then it stops.

It needs a conclusion, something to round it off, sum up the incident, deliver the punch line, hammer home the point, or whatever.

Another defect to be noticed is that though the lead is about little Tobias, leading the reader to believe this is a story about someone named Tobias Gravergaard, most of the rest of the piece, beginning in the third paragraph, is about Tobias's mother. The writer changed perspective.

Choosing the Perspective

A brite, and any other story as short as a brite, should be told from one perspective only. In the case of the police car brite, for example, the story was told from the perspective of Nanci Gustafson, and the reader sees everything just as Nanci saw it.

To tell the story entirely from little Tobias's perspective, the writer would have, in effect, had the reader tumble out of the car with Tobias, and the scene would have been at the shoulder of the road, with Eva Gravergaard's car disappearing into the distance while other cars were stopping, their drivers and passengers approaching Tobias and attending to him as he sat there.

Instead, the scene remains the interior of the car while little Tobias suddenly vanishes from the reader's view. The reader doesn't learn what's happened to Tobias until his mother finds out.

The little Tobias story actually is, and should have been written as, Eva Gravergaard's story. It is the story of a young mother who—horrifying thought!—loses her little boy from the back seat of her speeding car. The writer should have let the reader get into mom's head and feel the experience from her perspective. That perspective fits the facts in the brite, so the reader's identification is with the adult in the piece. Adult readers will much more readily identify with the mother, feel her fright and anxiety, then relief, than they will identify with a seven-year-old boy.

Every writer, in every case, must be careful to choose the best way to tell the story, and that especially includes the perspective from which the story will be told.

Writing the Lead

One other important thing should be noticed about the little Tobias brite. It has a specific-statement lead. What is said in the lead is said about only one person: little Tobias Gravergaard.

The police car lead, on the other hand, is a general-statement lead. It's about nobody in particular, but everybody in general.

Specific-statement leads can have a tendency to screen out readers when they are as brief as a brite lead must be. They have a way of subtly telling the reader, "This doesn't pertain to you; you don't have to read it." For example, whereas the little Tobias lead makes no connection to the reader, the police car lead makes a statement that virtually any reader can relate to, because it's within the scope of his experience. If possible then, the writer should write a brite lead that makes a general statement.

The brite lead should perform a couple of additional tasks: (1) provoke the reader's interest, one of the ordinary functions of any lead; and (2) set up the reader for the point of the story, which he will get if he reads the whole brite. The reader thus will see the same irony, humor, or great oddity that the writer saw when he decided to write the story as a brite.

The lead certainly should also be terse and short, no more than one sentence usually, and no more than a paragraph ever.

Telling the Anecdote

There are four things to be said about the way the anecdote should be told:

1. It should be told *chronologically,* so the incident being related unfolds for the reader in the same order in which it occurred in reality. When quotes are used in the anecdote, they should be only those quotes that occurred within the context of the action.

2. It should be told *clearly.* The reader needs enough detail and information to clearly see and understand the action, situation, and characters being described.

3. It must be told *concisely.* The writer needs to provide enough words to make the situation and action clear, but no more than necessary. The entire story must be told quickly.

4. It needs to be *aimed* at the point of the brite. Just as a joke must be told in a certain way in order for its listener or reader to get it, a brite must also be told with the effect of leading the reader to get the point—the same point of irony, humor, or great oddity the writer saw in the incident he's now relating to the reader.

Writing the Conclusion

Anybody can make a mistake.

When a passer-by saw a human form floating in a pool of stagnant water in a landfill in the 3400 block of North Collins about 11 a.m. Friday, he called the police.

Police, in turn, dispatched their most somber crew, the homicide squad, and they, too, saw a forlorn figure, drifting, partially submerged, in the foul water.

The detectives could not reach the figure, however. So they secured a small boat and paddled out through the muck.

What they found was a mannequin.

"I guess somebody had thrown it away. That's a garbage dump anyway," a police dispatcher said.

The lead of that brite, which ran in the *Dallas Morning News,* introduced the idea of people, or a person, making a mistake. "Mistake" is the key idea.

The reader is thus led to believe the story he is about to read is about somebody making a mistake. The lead makes a general statement, is somewhat provocative, is terse, and sets up the point of the brite. The brite's going well so far.

Then comes the anecdote recreating the incident. It's told chronologically, clearly, and concisely and is aimed at the point of the story—a mistake being made. The anecdote is told mostly from one perspective. The reader sees the passer-by and the scene, precisely described, and follows the action to the police, then sees the rest of the action, scene, and characters from the viewpoint of the police.

Then the reader, at exactly the appropriate spot in the unfolding of the story, sees the mistake:

What they found was a mannequin.

The reader gets it. The lead, which set up the point, now makes sense. The brite is going really well.

Since the anecdote, part two of the outline, is ended, the piece now needs a conclusion to round it off, sum up the point, or deliver the punch line:

"I guess somebody had thrown it away. That's a garbage dump anyway," a police dispatcher said.

That's a conclusion all right—a quote that constitutes a comment on the incident, delivered after the action had ended. But it is a poor conclusion because it fails to round off the story or sum up the point or deliver a punch line.

To be successful, the conclusion should refer to the idea introduced in the lead—in this case the key idea of a mistake. Instead, the concluding quote merely provides the reader a reason for the mannequin's having been in the landfill. The writer needed a quote that included the idea of "mistake," something, ideally, that pointed out the similarity between a mannequin and a body.

Using such an out-of-the-context-of-the-action quote is probably the best way to conclude a brite. It helps authenticate the story and it permits the writer to put a voice into the piece. But for the brite to be well done, the concluding quote should say something appropriate. It should refer to the idea introduced in the lead, as the conclusion in the police car brite does. There the concluding quote reinforces the idea of the irony of police being disturbers, rather than protectors, of the peace. The piece is thereby rounded off, the point summed up, the punch line delivered. Here it is again.

The lead.

> Police are not only protectors of our community, but can also be disturbers of our peace.

The conclusion.

> "I always thought police were supposed to stop disturbances," Nanci said, "not cause them."

In that example, it's clear to the reader that he's reached the end, exactly the effect sought by the writer.

Sometimes the writer can purposely elicit the needed quote. For example, if the writer of the mannequin brite had known what his lead was to say, he could have asked the police dispatcher (his apparent source), "Did the detectives really think it was a dead body?" Or, "Were the detectives actually fooled by the mannequin?"—or something else that would be likely to produce a quote suited to the lead.

However, in actual practice, the writer is usually stuck with whatever the source first said. He has to make do with what he's got. To solve his problem, he must choose the concluding quote first, then write a lead to conform to it. For example, the writer of the mannequin brite could have written a lead to introduce the idea of "dump" or "throw away" or "garbage," any of which would tie in with the concluding quote. Here's how it might have been done, changing nothing but the lead:

> It was a perfect spot to dispose of a body.
>
> When a passer-by saw a human form floating in a pool of stagnant water in a landfill in the 3400 block of North Collins about 11 a.m. Friday, he called the police.
>
> Police, in turn, dispatched their most somber crew, the homicide squad, and they, too, saw a forlorn figure, drifting, partially submerged, in the foul water.
>
> The detectives could not reach the figure, however. So they secured a small boat and paddled out though the muck.
>
> What they found was a mannequin.
>
> "I guess somebody had thrown it away. That's a garbage dump anyway," a police dispatcher said.

Ordinarily, the writer cannot control a quote. He must use it verbatim or with an ellipsis, or not at all. He can't change someone else's words. But the lead is formed from the writer's words, not from his source's. His total control of the lead means he may write it to fit the facts and the brite's requirements to achieve the effect desired.

The Basic Brite

Brites provide the developing writer a matchless instrument on which to practice his skill.

When the writer has gathered the facts and knows there's a story in them, his remaining task is to tell the story well. Since the brite is as short as it is, it lets him cast and recast the story, boil it down, say it clearly, make it make the point, revise until the piece comes out precisely right—never exceeding a page of copy, however.

The brite is like a single cell. Everything that makes a piece of writing is in it: narrative, description, quotes, exposition. The big difference between it and a grander piece is length. Additional length means simply more material. Grander pieces are in essence the same as brites; there's just more to them.

Mastering the art of telling a story to make a point—exactly the requirement of a well done brite—is the key to successful writing.

Fifty Writing Rules, Hints, and Points to Remember

IF I WERE TO READ YOUR MANUSCRIPTS, carefully going through them and making notes, I'm certain the items to be discussed in a critique would include most of the ones below. As an editor and teacher of writers, I've found these represent the most frequently recurring troubles in features and articles. Some constitute big writing problems, some not so big, some rather small. These rules, hints, and points to note are all important in crafting a well-told story.

Angle

1. Make sure you see the angle clearly before you start writing the piece. You should be able to sum up the idea of the piece in six to nine words. Fill in the blanks: It's a piece about _____ _____ _____ _____ _____; or it's the story of _____ _____ __ _____ _____ _____.
If you can't do it in less than ten words, you probably don't have the angle clear in your head.

Organization

2. Put the character's description in one place. Introduce a character so the reader sees the whole person at the time of the introduction, as he would if he met the character in person. Avoid dismembering the character and scattering his or her parts throughout the piece, with eye color in one paragraph, weight four paragraphs later, and a mustache three paragraphs after that.

Language

3. Use simple, straightforward language. Plain English ordinarily says it best. Write to communicate, not to impress.

4. Avoid using "this" as a subject, for clarity's sake.

5. Avoid wordiness. Don't use three or four words when one or two will do ("at this point in time," for example, instead of "now").

6. Use "that" to refer to something or someone already mentioned, in a preceding sentence or paragraph. Use "this" to refer to something or someone yet to be mentioned, in a succeeding sentence or paragraph.

7. Know that "explained" is not a synonym for "said." It must not be used as one, as in:

> "Kiss me," she explained.

8. Use all attribution words carefully. "Said," "told," and "asked" ordinarily are the words that say it best. Others serve the primary purpose of avoiding repetition. Guard against such attributions as:

> "I love it here," he smiled.

He didn't smile that statement; he *said* it, smiling. Other attribution words to watch include: "added" (he didn't add it; he said it); "quipped" (it should be clear from the quote and the context that he was quipping; you shouldn't have to tell the reader the quote was a quip); "joked"; "laughed"; "hissed" (appropriate only with sibilant sounds); "admitted" (use only when it fits the dictionary definition); "remembered" (it tends to destroy the chronology by shifting perspective from then to now).

9. Avoid use of "very." It's a vague crutch word in most cases. Pick words that say something specific to the reader.

10. Avoid use of "lady" when you mean "woman." The same, of course, goes for "gentleman" when you mean "man," but in contrast to "lady," there is no tendency among writers to call men "gentlemen."

11. Avoid use of "you" and "your." In some cases, speaking personally to the reader and addressing him or her as "you" is the effect desired (as in this chapter). Unless it is a special case, however, avoid the conversational "you."

12. Avoid redundancies. "He shrugged his shoulders." What else can a person shrug but his shoulders? The "his shoulders" is redundant. Leave it out. "She nodded her head in agreement." Her head is the only part of her she could nod; you needn't include "her head." "He thought to himself." How else could he think? Use either "he said to himself," if the words were spoken, or simply "he thought."

13. Avoid tritenesses and clichés. Unless you're trying for a special effect, don't use tired, old expressions: "face the future," "twinkle in his

eyes," "coast to coast," "bottom line," "Pandora's box," "shadow of the goal post," "let's face it," "the buck stops here," and other such phrases that have grown stale with time and overuse. Come up with your own similes, metaphors, and colorful expressions.

14. Know the differences between "most" and "many." A generalization such as "most people today" or "most doctors agree that" must be supported by a survey or other documentation. "Most" means "the greatest number." Its use requires more than a writer's guess. "Many," on the other hand, is less sweeping and much safer to use accurately. "Some" and "few" are likewise words to be used precisely to express imprecise numbers and amounts.

15. Use "hopefully" only according to its dictionary definition. It means "full of hope," not "I hope."

Quotes

16. Avoid so-what quotes. This so-what quote is from a UPI story about the brother of baseball pitcher Pascual Perez, who got lost trying to leave the Atlanta airport:

> When told his brother got lost, he closed his eyes and said: "Oh, man."

Here's another:

> GAU chief negotiator Randy Rutsky said the agreement is "a significant step forward."

17. Avoid ghostly quotes. They're the kind that leave the reader wondering who said it, as in these examples:

> A Chinese farmer known as "Charlie Two Shoes" to U.S. Marines who befriended him as a boy 37 years ago arrived in America yesterday and burst into tears of joy as he embraced one of his "old Marine buddies."

> The agreement, wrought only after several bouts with "heated tempers" on both sides of the bargaining table, will end with a guarantee that graduate assistants in Florida will get pay hikes, job security and workload provisions.

> The tools of Joel Davis' trade include a 94-mph fastball, an "awesome" slider, major-league curve and a knuckleball so good his coach won't let him throw it.

> Judge Peyton Miles has tried "fussing and cussing" at the parents of truant school children.

18. Attribute as often as necessary for clarity. It may not be necessary to attribute every quote if it's perfectly clear to the reader who the speaker is. Repeated attributions can become tiresome, awkward, and space consuming. Make sure that the speaker is clear to the reader; when in doubt, put in the attribution.

19. Place the attribution in an appropriate spot. Pick one of three possible locations:

At the end of the quote

> "This is positively the last time I'll ever set foot in Yankee Stadium. I've had it with those guys," Dixon said.

At the beginning of the quote

> Dixon said, "This is positively the last time I'll ever set foot in Yankee Stadium. I've had it with those guys."

Somewhere in between

> "This is positively the last time I'll ever set foot in Yankee Stadium," Dixon said. "I've had it with those guys."

Ordinarily, what the speaker of the quote said is more important and more interesting than the fact he said it. Therefore the quote generally should come before the attribution. In the above examples, the attribution is more appropriately placed at the end or in the middle of the quote. In such a short quote it probably doesn't matter whether the attribution is at the end or in the middle. However, in a long quote—several lines of type—the reader shouldn't be made to wait till the quote ends to discover who said it. Therefore, the appropriate place for the attribution in a long quote is a spot no deeper in the quote than the middle—perhaps at the end of the first sentence. For example:

> "If anything stuck in my mind during the training class that morning, it was the importance of guarding the ripcord on my reserve parachute," Sandra said. "A ripcord wasn't necessary for the main chute, which was strapped to my back. It was attached to a static line and would open automatically when I jumped out of the plane.
> "But if the reserve cord were accidentally pulled while I was still inside the plane, the force of the chute catching the wind rushing through the cabin could pull me right through the wall of the fuselage."

In some cases, the fact that a certain person said the quote is as important or interesting as the quote itself. In such cases, the appropriate spot for the attribution might be at the beginning. For example, if George Steinbrenner, the owner of the Yankees, had made the quote about Yankee Stadium, the attribution would be appropriately placed this way:

> Steinbrenner then said, "This is positively the last time I'll ever set foot in Yankee Stadium. I've had it with those guys."

Look for the best spot in which to place the attribution—for effect or clarity or both.

Grammar

20. Use past tense. Sometimes, for some special effect, present tense is a good choice, but in most cases past tense does the job better. For example, in a piece written in past tense, using the word *answers* indicates the speaker gives the same answer every time he is asked the question:

> "That's the way the government sees it," he answers. "But it's not the way I look at it."

What does *answers* indicate if the piece is written in present tense? The language's precision is lost in such a case.

Many writers choose present tense because they harbor the mistaken idea that present tense makes the action seem more immediate. Actually, however, action occurs and events unfold to the reader at exactly the same rate in past tense as they do in present tense. To test that statement, read a narrative passage in past tense and notice that though the verbs indicate past action in the writing, the action is current in your mind as you read.

21. Stick with one tense. Whether you choose past or, for some special reason, present tense, be consistent throughout the piece: Make it all past or all present.

22. Put subject before verb. Except in rare, special cases, modern English usage places the subject before the verb. You should, too. Write it, "O'Malley said," "the sheriff reported," "Caldwell asked." Avoid the common newspaper practice of inverting subject and verb: "said O'Malley," "reported the sheriff," "asked Caldwell."

To judge just how stilted and silly such inversions are, try putting verb before subject in your conversations or try inverting using a pronoun

instead of a noun: "said she," "asked he," "reported she."
Handle appositives like this:

> "I didn't know how sick he was,"
> Gerald Bauer, the minister who be-
> friended Gilbert, said.

23. Use active, rather than passive, voice if possible. Make the subject of the sentence act, rather than be acted upon. For example, write

> The cow's owner roped it and threw
> it to the ground."

instead of

> The cow was roped and thrown to
> the ground by its owner.

Spelling

24. *A lot* is two words, not one.

25. Know the difference between *its* and *it's* and use the correct one. If the sentence makes sense when the words *it is* are inserted, then use *it's*. If not, then you want the possessive *its*.

26. Learn to form the plural and possessive of proper nouns. The James B. Roberts family is the James B. Robertses. The Albert Diaz family is the Albert Diazes. The residence that belongs to the James B. Roberts family is the Robertses' house. The car that belongs to Albert Diaz's family is the Diazes' car. The hat that belongs to James B. Roberts is Roberts' hat or Roberts's hat. (In the latter example, a good rule to follow in deciding whether to add an *s* is to speak the word and if in speaking it, you pronounce an extra syllable, add the *s*.)

27. If you're not sure how a word is spelled, look it up.

Punctuation

28. Remember that punctuation is important and treat it accordingly.

Details

29. Don't summarize scenes, dialogue, or action. Recreate them. Let the reader see for himself. Let the characters speak for themselves.

30. Be specific; avoid vagueness.

31. Show; don't tell. Insofar as possible, always let the reader see

something—scenes, action, people, detail. Use exposition only when absolutely necessary.

32. Identify the characters. When introducing a character, give some information about him or her—age, address or home town, occupation—to let the reader know him or her better.

33. Describe the characters. Let the reader get some idea of what they look like.

34. Include important detail. Let the reader see for himself, but don't show him irrelevant objects or insignificant details. They mislead the reader, clutter the manuscript, and use up valuable space in the piece.

Editorializing

35. Stick to facts. Ordinarily, your job as a writer is to present observable fact—what a person would have seen, heard, felt, smelled had he been at the scene at the time the reality occurred. Avoid editorializing, making judgments, delivering opinions, and offering evaluations. Instead of writing, "The crowd went wild," for example, recreate the scene and let the reader draw the conclusion that the crowd went wild. Instead of writing, "Campo was shabbily dressed," describe his clothes and let the reader decide.

36. Don't puff the subject. The piece is meant to report the subject, not praise it. The piece is not to be any kind of payment or gratuity for information received or interview granted. The writer shouldn't feel he owes his source anything but accuracy and fairness. His foremost obligation is neither to his source nor subject, but to his readers.

Style

37. Call people by their names or use appropriate pronouns. Once you've introduced and described the characters, refer to them by their names, as you would do in conversation. Don't refer to them as, for example, "the sophomore quarterback" or "the blue-eyed singer" or "the former attorney."

38. Be natural with names. Let the circumstances determine whether a person in the piece should be called by first name, last name, or last name and title. "Susan" sounds right for a two-year-old, even a 17-year-old, but it doesn't sound right for someone 64 years old. "Cohen" sounds okay for a 30-year-old man, but not for a 12-year-old of either sex and probably not for a 30-year-old woman. Decide each case separately.

39. Don't be cute. Let the material carry the story, not cleverness. Most pieces depend for success on what the writer has to say, not how he says it.

40. Avoid asking questions. It's the answer that is important or in-

teresting, not the question. In most cases, the question is superfluous since the answer alone usually provides the information to the reader. For example:

> Why does Pettigrew risk his life for such a relatively small prize?
> "I don't do it for the money," he said. "Lord knows, there's not enough prize money to make it worth the risk. I do it 'cause I love to race—race anything, bikes, go-karts, cars, boats, horses, you name it. I just like to race."

Delete the question and write it like this:

> "I don't do it for the money," Pettigrew said. "Lord knows, there's not enough prize money to make it worth the risk. I do it 'cause I love to race—race anything, bikes, go-karts, cars, boats, horses, you name it. I just like to race."

Or like this:

> Pettigrew has his own reason for racing. "I don't do it for the money," he said. "Lord knows, there's not enough prize money to make it worth the risk. I do it 'cause I love to race—race anything, bikes, go-karts, cars, boats, horses, you name it. I just like to race."

41. Vary sentence structure and length. Don't build all your sentences the same way. All of anything is too much.

42. Make anecdotes make a point.

Mechanics

43. Keep paragraphs short. Don't make them choppy, but don't let them run on and on. Reading is hard work; long paragraphs make it even harder.

44. If you're writing as a freelance, put your byline on the piece.

45. Number the pages of your manuscript.

46. Make and keep a copy of the manuscript.

General Principles

47. Always see the reader as someone to be courted and won over.

48. To write really good, effective and memorable pieces, go for the

reader's heart, not his head.

49. When in doubt about whether to include or exclude material, put it in. It's infinitely easier for an editor to remove unwanted material than it is for him to add wanted material. If you're not sure, put it in and let the editor decide.

50. Edit your own piece. Let it—and yourself—cool off a bit, then carefully go back over it, looking for ways to make it better, clearer, and stronger.

One Final Word

THERE is probably no rule of writing that can't, on an appropriate occasion, be set aside. There's no form or formula that can't be replaced by something more effective when the conditions are exactly right.

The test of a piece of writing, after all, is not "Does it follow the rules?" Rather, it is "Does it work?" If it works, the rules and form don't really matter.

However, beginning writers' judgment as to what works and what doesn't needs time—and accumulated experiences of success and failure—to develop. New writers ordinarily need the discipline of following the rules and formulas whether they want to or not. Usually, the rules help the piece work, increasing its likelihood of success. They've become rules because in most cases they produce better results.

Writing, though, should be like the English language itself—not a tethered balloon, but a live bird, free and going wherever caprice and the forces of nature take it. The purpose of this book is not to restrict flight but to aid it. It deals with the fundamentals of nonfiction writing. A writer's learning them is like a fledgling's learning to fly. Once the fundamentals are mastered, his ability and energy are the only limits to what he can accomplish.

INDEX

BENTON RAIN PATTERSON was formerly editor of the Slidell, Louisiana, *Weekly News;* general assignment reporter on the Picayune, Mississippi, *Item;* sports editor of the Lawton, Oklahoma, *Morning Press;* wire editor of the Montgomery, Alabama, *Advertiser;* swing desk editor of the New Orleans, Louisiana, *States* and the St. Louis, Missouri, *Globe-Democrat;* staff writer and articles editor on *The Saturday Evening Post;* articles editor on *The New York Times Magazine;* staff writer on *The New York Times;* editor of *Dominion* magazine; and managing editor of *Guideposts* magazine.

He has been a freelance contributor to more than a dozen consumer and trade magazines. He was winner of a Jesse H. Neal Award for Editorial Achievement, presented by American Business Press for his article covering the 1967 race riots in Newark, New Jersey. He now teaches writing and magazine editing at the University of Florida.